# Baking at High Altitude

## The Muffin Lady's Old Fashioned Recipes

Please note that it is important to read the "Tips for Baking at High Altitude and for Using the Following Recipes" on page xi and the instructions for each recipe.

**This book is published by:**

The Muffin Lady Inc.

1532 Yankee Creek Road

Evergreen, CO 80439

For any questions concerning the preparation for any of the recipes from the following pages, please e-mail the Muffin Lady at: muffinchic@earthlink.net

ISBN 0-9745008-0-1

This book is

dedicated in loving

Memory of

My Grandmom

and

My Father

and to

all the Customers

on My Route.

# Table of Contents

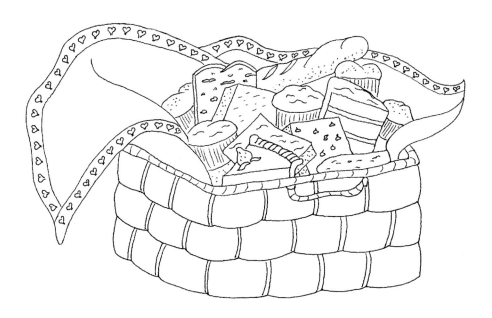

# Acknowledgments

I would first like to thank my Grandmom, for teaching me how to bake and for her love, support and endless knowledge about how to prepare the perfect baked treat. I also thank my Father, Len Levin, for his emotional support and belief in The Muffin Lady.

My everlasting appreciation, to all who shared their recipes with me: My Mother, my Aunt Lil Gomberg, my Aunt Lil's Mother and her Aunt, Kathleen Gebhardt, Cid Haas, Bubba from Kentucky, Cheryl Bezio Gorham, Bob Jackson, Carl Bowersox, Patt Roscoe and, of course, my Great Grandmom.

I wish to express my sincere admiration to my editor Hassell Bradley Wright, creative designer Kimberlee Lynch and proofreader Kelly Kordes Anton, for their patience, expertise, smiles and faith in The Muffin Lady.

I also thank Terry Erbert, a dear friend, who found me my wonderful editor, Hassell Bradley Wright.

A very special basketful of thanks to:

Dr. Kevin Lilliheu and his secretary Susan Clark
Dr. Chester Ridgeway
Dr. Maggie Weirman
Dr. Paul Wexler
Dr. Leonard Zemmel

I thank you for your patience and care with me. Without you, my doctors, I would not be here today to share all of these recipes.

*There is one extraordinary*

*ingredient that goes into everything that*

*I bake. Please do not forget this ingredient,*

*for it is imperative to all baking.*

*Whenever I bake,*

*I add extra spoonfuls of Love*

*to all of my recipes.*

*Love added to all things good,*

*makes them just a little bit better.*

# Introduction

I must have been 4. I was living with my parents in the suburbs just outside of Philadelphia. Already, I was learning to appreciate the emotional satisfaction that comes from baking, serving, sharing and eating freshly made baked treats right out of the oven.

Dolls never fascinated me; rather, my favorite toy was an Easy Bake Oven. I would be thrilled when my Dad actually ate and enjoyed the chocolate cakes I made for him. I quickly learned the persuasive power of a well-mixed batter, a light-as-a-feather cake, a good cookie and, of course, a muffin.

Sometimes I spent the night at my Grandmom's house when my parents went out. My Grandmom was my Father's Mother, and she possessed a Tin Box, which, to my childish eyes, seemed magical. It was this special Tin Box, full of treasured recipes, from which she taught me to bake. Frequently we laughed, and sometimes I was permitted, to my delight, to "take a taste."

Often, I would push a stool across the floor, and then I would climb up onto the counter to get a really good look. More often than not, Grandmom obliged me with a smile. She taught me to bake, using a scoop of this, a pinch of that and another spoonful of this. I will forever cherish her lessons in measurement. As a result of those precious lessons, I grew to learn that I was instructed by one of the finest bakers I have ever known. Now, many years later, I find her Tin Box to not only be bottomless, but also to be priceless.

I continued to bake while growing up, and often, I was requested to bake many of the recipes that I have included in this book. Eventually, I baked professionally.

At the age of 17, I moved to Colorado to go to college. I have never really left the state except to acquire one of my two graduate degrees. Because of my love of baking, I quickly learned how to adjust many East Coast baking recipes to a higher altitude, or at least 4,000 feet above the ocean, where the air is much thinner and drier. These adjustments became necessary, for I continued to bake for family and friends.

For 16 to 17 years, I taught and counseled children. I would almost always lure them with fresh, homemade baked goods to encourage them to get their work or goals accomplished on time. Without the high-altitude adjustments, my cookies would be too flat and my cakes and brownies would sink in the middle to the bottom of the pan.

For the last 17 years, I have lived at almost 8,000 feet above sea level, and the adjustments have become easy. I left my career due to medical and health reasons. During a stay at the hospital, a neighbor watched my home and animals for me. She would not accept any offer of money for her efforts, so I baked her a batch of oatmeal raisin cookies. She thought that they were so good, she suggested that I market them.

I needed something to do, at least part-time, so I looked in my Grandmom's Tin Box for a muffin recipe, found a superb muffin recipe and took samples to a local coffee shop. Soon after, I found myself delivering several kinds of baked treats every few days, not only to coffee shops and convenience stores, but to individual businesses around my home in Evergreen, Colorado.

These businesses became "My Route," and I continued to bring them baked treats several days a week for many years. I will always be grateful to these customers, for they were my guinea pigs, my friends and my regular customers. They gave me a smile and said, "Ah! You made the good stuff."

I will be eternally grateful to the United States Postal Service employees in Evergreen, Colorado, for they are the persons who gave me the title of "The Muffin Lady." Whenever I showed up, someone (usually Dan) would holler, "Muffin Lady's Here!" That became my business name.

After a year of baking for "My Route," I decided to venture out into the city of Denver. I called the LoDo Tattered Cover Bookstore in Denver and told them I sold great baked goods and brought them samples. Soon after, I left a note with the manager of a new Wild Oats Natural Marketplace, and I baked for these and various other commercial accounts in the city for a number of years.

Over the years, I have been asked for this or that recipe, and now the time has come for me to share them with all of you. The uniqueness of these recipes is that they were written from scratch baking for an altitude of 4,000 feet or more above sea level. Some cooks consider baking at high altitude an art, but with this book, you will learn how to succeed each time you bake. In other words, you will get the hang of it with my guidance and instructions.

It is my hope that you will find that baking at high altitude is not as difficult as you might think. Much time and effort was applied to adjusting recipes from friends and family members. It is remarkable that these adjustments never changed the taste. Some of these recipes will be low fat, some laced with butter. Some of the ingredients can be substituted to meet dietary needs. Many of the recipes have been tried and tested by a number of generations and then served to a great variety of people. In other words, they are genuinely old-fashioned recipes, shared by many generations and now to be shared with you and for generations to come.

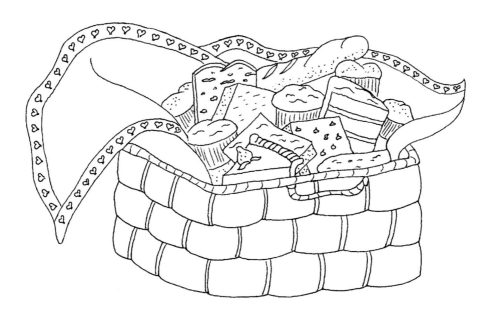

# Tips for Baking at High Altitude

*and for Using the Following Recipes*

*Be prepared to hear many different versions for high altitude baking requirements.*
*All of the recipes in this book have been tried and tested many times.*

- For recipes that are lower in cholesterol and/or fat look, for a ♥ under the recipe title.

- For recipes that can be made with a sugar substitute (hence sugar free), look for a **SUGAR FREE** under the recipe title.

- All the recipes are to be prepared with an electric mixer unless specified otherwise.

- You may have been told to decrease or increase the baking soda and/or baking powder by ¼. I do not. What I do when measuring these two leavening agents is to make sure the amount is not measured to the top of the measuring spoon, but just a tiny bit below the top of the measuring spoon. To do this, when measuring the leavening agent, indent your finger into the ingredient a tiny speck when leveling the measuring spoon.

- Many people have suggested to me over the years that when baking at High Altitude it is necessary to decrease the amount of sugar by 1-4 teaspoons per cup. Keep in mind that sugar adds moisture to the majority of recipes. Although, I appreciate and will always welcome suggestions, I have found through much trial and effort that when measuring sugar, make sure that the amount is just a pinch below the cup line in a measuring cup and never above the cup line.

- Whenever a recipe in this book calls for oats, please use quick-cooking oats for the recipes. Old-fashioned oats suck-up more moisture in a baked product as compared to quick-cooking oats.

- In several recipes in this book, you can substitute white or brown for an amount of sugar-free substitute. I prefer to use either Twin or Splenda as my substitutes. The decision about what kind of substitute to use is yours. Please consider that sugar substitutes have a tendency to be very sweet, so if you want to decrease the amount of your chosen substitute, do so by about 1 tablespoon per ½ cup, but not more, or you may have a dry batter and a dry batch of treats.

- I have learned that using canola oil in some of the recipes is best for flavor and your health. Low in fat and cholesterol, canola oil helps keep treats moist, particularly in drier climates such as those in the Rocky Mountains.

- I have learned, through devilish trial and error adventures with my Grandmom's recipes, that the best way to adjust a recipe to high altitude is to increase the liquids (except oil) about 1½ tablespoons per 1 cup and to increase flour about 1½ tablespoons per 1 cup.

- Always test a baked product before removing it from the oven. Insert a clean knife or a toothpick into the center of a baked product and remove it carefully. If a crumb or several crumbs cling to the knife or toothpick, this means the product is not fully baked. Bake the product for a few more minutes. Although baking times are supplied, all ovens heat and cook differently, so the baking duration in my oven may be a few minutes different from yours.

- When rolling dough out onto flour, keep the flour usage to a minimum. If your dough continues to stick, place a sheet of waxed paper on the surface. Sprinkle a little flour onto the wax paper and then roll out the dough.

- Some recipes, when baking at high altitude, require an extra egg or two. I always bake with large or extra-large eggs. If using medium or smaller eggs, add an extra egg. The recipes on the following pages will state at the bottom of the page whether you should add an extra egg when doubling or tripling the amounts of ingredients in that specific recipe. At High Altitude an extra egg will assist the leavening agents (baking soda and baking powder) to make the dough rise.

- Always make sure your oven is preheated to the designated temperature before baking anything, unless specified otherwise.

- Most recipes require a greased baking pan. I have found that unflavored pan spray, butter or margarine work best when preparing a pan prior to adding a batter or dough.

- When baking at high altitude, **do not** use a piece of parchment paper on a cookie sheet when baking cookies, as many recipes (not found in this book) suggest. Instead, spray the pan with pan spray or butter the pan. The parchment paper will only suck up extra moisture from your cookies, which you really do not want to happen.

- Some of the best tips I have learned and can share with you, specifically when baking in drier climates (Colorado, Arizona, New Mexico, Wyoming, Nevada and Utah) that are at high altitude, are about how to handle the product, once fully baked and removed from the oven. Read the following sections for these tips.

MUFFINS

There are three sizes of muffin pan sections that I use for most of my muffin recipes. A large muffin pan section is about 3½ inches across the top, the regular size muffin pan section is about 2½ inches across the top and the mini muffin pan section is about 1-1½ inches across the top of each muffin section.

Remove the fully baked muffins from the pan within 1-2 minutes after removing from the oven. This is to prevent any further cooking in the hot pan. Wrap each muffin individually (except for mini muffins) in cellophane within 5-10 minutes after removing from the pan. Or, place two to four regular size muffins or mini muffins into a Ziploc bag to seal in the moisture. If serving the muffins shortly after removal from the oven, place them on a plate and cover the entire plate with cellophane until served.

COOKIES

Once cookies are fully baked and removed from the oven, let them cool for 5-6 minutes. Then, you can either wrap them in cellophane or place them in a Ziploc bag sealed for freshness. I usually wrap the larger cookies (4-5 inches) individually in cellophane. If using a decorative can, layer the bottom of the can with waxed paper or cellophane, fill with cookies, and then cover with cellophane and make sure the lid for the can fits snuggly so no air can get in. If serving cookies shortly after removal from the oven, place them on a plate and cover with cellophane. By the way, I have discovered that Shortbread Cookies will stay fresh the longest compared to all the cookie recipes in these pages, and they do not need to be immediately covered with cellophane.

CAKES

Usually, it is best to let cakes cool in the pan, unless specified differently. However, you will want to cover the cake completely with cellophane within 7 minutes after removal from the oven to lock in the moisture rather than letting it evaporate. To serve a coffeecake warm is fine, but let it cool for at least 10 minutes prior to cutting the cake into pieces. For a layer cake, wrap each layer in cellophane and let each layer cool completely until you are ready to apply the icing.

BREADS

Within 2-3 minutes of removing them from the oven, remove each individual loaf from the pan to prevent any further baking. Let the loaf cool for another 2-4 minutes, and then wrap in cellophane to seal in all the moisture. If serving shortly after removal from the oven, allow to cool for 10 minutes, slice into six to seven pieces (more slices will begin to fall apart while hot) and put the slices on a plate or into a bread basket lined with wax paper and/or linen lined with waxed paper.

BROWNIES

Once fully baked and removed from the oven, let them cool for 4-5 minutes and then cover the pan with cellophane. Most brownies can be cut into pieces and served after cooling 10 minutes, unless specified otherwise.

Always keep brownies tightly covered in the pan when not serving. **Do not** cut brownies into individual pieces while storing them in the pan as that will dry them out more quickly; slice only the amount of pieces being served. If you are taking them somewhere without the pan, first cut them, and then wrap them individually in cellophane, place them in a plastic container with a lid or place them on a plate covered tightly with cellophane.

## FRUIT BARS, COBBLERS, CRISPS

After fully cooked and removed from the oven, let them cool for about 10 minutes and then cover the pan or dish with cellophane to keep the moisture in the product. Let the bars cool for 5-10 minutes prior to serving or you may burn you tongue. To take fruit bars somewhere, cut them into individual pieces and then wrap each piece in cellophane, place them in a plastic container with a lid or place them on a plate covered tightly with cellophane to keep them fresh and moist. Make sure you cover any remaining product tightly with cellophane. If serving a cobbler or crisp shortly after removal from the oven, you do not need to cover the pan with cellophane. Fruit bars do not need to be kept chilled.

All cobblers and crisps need to be refrigerated once they are completely cool. To reheat a cobbler or crisp, cover the fruit-filled dish or pan with foil and heat at the original baking temperature for 10 minutes or dish out the desired amount and reheat it in the microwave.

## PIES

Pies are easy: you simply need to let them cool for a bit prior to eating. When transporting a pie, please cover it with cellophane or place it in a plastic container. Crème pies should be kept refrigerated until ready to serve. Unless you have a very cold refrigerator, place the whipped cream on top of the cream filling just prior to serving or the cream may lose its fluffy consistency and look as if it has melted.

## STRUDELS

Always let strudels cool 30 percent through prior to serving (except for baked Brie); this prevents you from burning your mouth and it holds the strudel together better. When storing strudel, I always wrap it tightly in cellophane after it is 75 percent cool. If you wrap puff pastry dough too soon after removal from the oven, it has a tendency to lose a lot of its flakiness, especially with strudels.

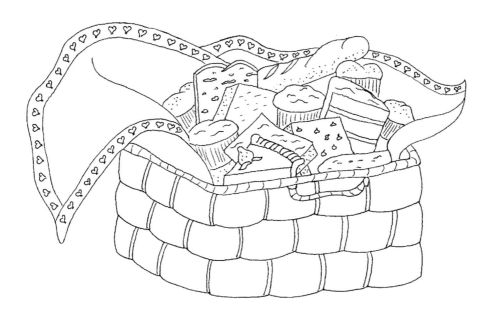

# Baking at High Altitude

## The Muffin Lady's Old Fashioned Recipes

# The Value of a Smile

The thing that goes the farthest

That costs the least and does the most,

Is just a pleasant Smile

It's full of mirth and goodness,

With heavenly kindness blest;

It's worth a billion dollars

And doesn't cost a cent

I have much optimism that the use of the recipes within these pages

Will get you many, many smiles.

*The Muffin Lady*

# Cookies

* Note that all recipes can be doubled or tripled.
* You must use softened butter or margarine for all cookies unless stated otherwise.
* Always keep cookies in a sealed bag or a tightly topped can, lined and topped with wax paper or cellophane, or wrapped in cellophane to keep them fresh.

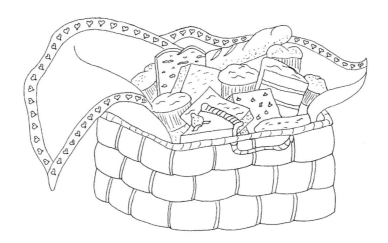

**Clockwise from top:** Large Snickerdoodles
Almond Chocolate Chip, Chocolate Chip,
Shortbread, Shortbread Sandwiches, Rugalach

**Center:** Snickerdoodles, Thumbprint,
Spritz Cookies

# Chocolate-Chip Cookies

*I have been baking these cookies since I was 8 years old. Occasionally, when I came home from school*
*in the afternoons, my Mother and her friends would ask me to bake them up a batch. Many years later, men*
*at a local bar paid me $20 to bake them up a batch. Now, more than 15 years after my barfly days,*
*I continue to receive requests to bake these cookies for friends and customers.*

**30 plus small or 7-8 large cookies**

Preheat oven to 350 degrees F.

1 cup (2 sticks) butter
1 tablespoon vanilla
¾ cup minus 1 tablespoon sugar
¾ cup plus 2 tablespoons brown sugar
2 eggs
2½ cups plus 1 tablespoon flour
⅞ teaspoon baking soda
1½ cups chocolate chips
¾ cups chopped walnuts (optional)

1. Cream together the butter, vanilla and sugars.
2. Add the remaining ingredients to the butter mixture and mix thoroughly.
3. Grease 2 cookie sheets.
4. Drop dough by tablespoonful or with small ice cream scoop onto the prepared cookie sheets. For larger cookies (4-5 inches) use ⅓ cup of dough and slightly flatten each large cookie with the palm of your hand.
5. Bake smaller cookies 7-9 minutes or until brown around the edges. Bake larger cookies 9-12 minutes or until brown around the edges.

# Chipper Chocolate-Chip Cookies

*This recipe is a fabulous alternative to the traditional chocolate-chip cookie. A friend of mine received this recipe from a friend and passed it on to me. Since I received this recipe, it has been enjoyed by many. These are a perfect treat to take to a holiday office party.*

**30 plus cookies**

Preheat oven to 350 degrees F.

1 cup (2 sticks) butter
¾ cup sugar
¾ cup brown sugar
2 eggs
1 tablespoon vanilla
1-1½ tablespoons Frangelica
1-1½ tablespoons Kahlua or Grand Mariner
2⅔ cups flour
1 teaspoon baking soda
1½ cups chocolate chips or 2 cups mini chocolate chips
½ cup chopped pecans or walnuts
½ cup chopped macadamia nuts or hazelnuts

1. Cream together the butter, sugars, eggs, vanilla, Frangelica and Kahlua.

2. Add the remaining ingredients. Mix the ingredients thoroughly.

3. Grease 2 cookie sheets.

4. Drop dough by tablespoonful for each cookie onto prepared cookie sheets.

5. Bake 7-10 minutes or until golden brown around the edges.

# Chris's Favorite Oatmeal Cookies

*These were my Father's and are my friend Chris's favorite cookies I baked for them—soft in the middle, crunchy on the edges, with just the right amount of spice. These were the first popular items I sold to my soon-to-be regular customers.*

**36 plus small or 8-10 large cookies**

Preheat oven to 375 degrees F.

1 cup (2 sticks) margarine, melted
¼ cup (½ stick) butter or margarine
1 tablespoon vanilla
¾ cup plus 2 tablespoons brown sugar or brown sugar substitute
½ cup sugar or sugar substitute
3 cups plus 1½ tablespoons oatmeal
2 eggs or equivalent amount of liquid egg substitute
1½ cups plus 2 tablespoons flour
1 teaspoon baking soda
2 teaspoons cinnamon
½ teaspoon nutmeg
Additions if desired: chopped walnuts, pecans and/or raisins and/or chocolate chips; I like to use both dark and golden raisins

1. Cream together the butter, margarine, vanilla and sugars.

2. Add the remaining ingredients, adding 1 egg at a time while mixing. Mix all the ingredients thoroughly.

3. Grease 2 cookie sheets.

4. Drop dough by a tablespoonful or with a small ice cream scoop onto the prepared cookie sheets. For larger cookies (4-5 inches), drop ⅓ cup dough onto cookie sheets. Place each large cookie onto a prepared cookie sheet and slightly flatten it with the palm of your hand.

5. Bake smaller cookie 7-9 minutes. Bake larger cookies 12-14 minutes.

# Grandmom's Oatmeal Cookies

*This is my Grandmom's recipe for Oatmeal Cookies. These are much different from mine, but they taste just as wonderful. The choice of whose is better is a matter of personal taste. Try both, and you choose.*

**30 plus cookies**

Preheat oven to 375 degrees F.

1 ¾ cups flour
1 teaspoon baking soda
1 teaspoon salt
1 cup (2 sticks) butter
1 cup sugar
1 cup brown sugar
2 teaspoons vanilla
2 eggs
3 cups oats
2 teaspoons cinnamon
1 cup dark raisins
1 cup chocolate chips

1. Sift the flour, baking soda and salt into a small bowl and set aside.

2. Cream together the butter, sugars, vanilla and eggs. Add the sifted flour, oats, cinnamon, raisins and chocolate chips to the butter mixture. Mix all the ingredients thoroughly.

3. Grease 2 cookie sheets.

4. Use a tablespoonful or a small ice cream scoop to drop the dough onto the prepared cookie sheets.

5. Bake 8-10 minutes.

# Oatmeal Thumbprints

*This recipe was created because I wanted a healthier version of a jam-filled thumbprint cookie, which is ordinarily made with lots of butter and sugar. This recipe has a scrumptious, old-fashioned flavor, especially for a cookie that is a bit on the healthy side.*

**24 plus cookies**

Preheat oven to 350 degrees F.

1 cup (2 sticks) of margarine
½ cup plus 1 tablespoon brown sugar or brown sugar substitute
2 eggs or equivalent amount of liquid egg substitute
1 tablespoon vanilla
1½ cups plus 2 tablespoons flour
1½ cups oats
2 teaspoons cinnamon
½ teaspoon nutmeg
1 cup finely chopped nuts (I prefer walnuts)
⅓ cup jam or sugarless jam

1. Cream together the margarine, sugar, eggs and vanilla.

2. Add the flour, oats, cinnamon and nutmeg to the butter mixture. Mix all the ingredients together thoroughly.

3. Grease 2 cookie sheets.

4. Roll 1½ tablespoons of dough into a ball with the palms of your hands. Roll each ball in finely chopped nuts.

5. Indent the center of each ball with your thumb, and place it on a prepared cookie sheet. Fill each indent with ½-1 teaspoon of jam.

6. Bake 12-15 minutes, until golden brown.

# Peanut Butter Cookies

*I never had any complaints with this recipe. Actually, I get frequent requests for these cookies from special friends in faraway places. This recipe produces fantastic peanut butter cookies. Properly made, they are crunchy around the edges and soft in the middle.*

**30 plus small or 6-8 large cookies**

Preheat oven to 375 degrees F.

½ cup (1 stick) butter or margarine
½ cup plus 1 tablespoon brown sugar
½ cup sugar
1 tablespoon vanilla
2 eggs
1½ cups peanut butter (Do not use chunky peanut butter because at high altitude
 it can dry these cookies out quickly.)
1½ cups flour
½ teaspoon baking soda
Additions if desired: chocolate chips or raisins

1. Cream together the butter, sugars and vanilla.

2. Add the peanut butter and mix well.

3. Add the remaining ingredients, adding the eggs 1 at a time. Mix all the ingredients together thoroughly.

4. Grease 2 cookie sheets.

5. For smaller cookies, roll 1 tablespoon of dough into a ball and place onto prepared cookie sheet. Using a fork, make a crisscross design on top of each cookie. For larger cookies (3-4 inches), roll 1/3 cup dough into a ball using the palms of your hands, place onto prepared cookie sheets and flatten with a fork by making a crisscross design.

6. Bake smaller cookies 8-10 minutes or until brown around the edges. Bake larger cookies 10-12 minutes or until brown around the edges.

# Snickerdoodles

*If you want to impress those you love with a great cookie, here it is. They have been a favorite among my friends and customers for many years. My favorite boys on earth refer to these as "the perfect cookie."*

**36 plus small or 8-9 large cookies**

Preheat oven to 350 degrees F.

¾ cup sugar
3 tablespoons cinnamon
Mix these ingredients together and set aside in a small bowl.

1 cup (2 sticks) butter
1 cup sugar
1½ tablespoons vanilla
1 egg
2 cups plus 1 tablespoon flour
1 teaspoon baking powder
¼ teaspoon baking soda
⅛ teaspoon cream of tartar

1. Cream together the butter, sugar and vanilla.
2. Add the remaining ingredients, ending with the egg. Thoroughly mix all the ingredients for 2 minutes on medium-high.
3. Grease 2 cookie sheets.
4. For smaller cookies, roll 1 tablespoon of dough into a ball with the palms of your hands. For larger cookies (4-5 inches), roll ⅓ cup dough into a ball with the palms of your hands.

*continued on next page*

5. Roll each cookie in the cinnamon/sugar mixture, completely coating each cookie, and place onto prepared cookie sheets. Slightly flatten each cookie with the palm of your hand.

6. Bake smaller cookies 7-10 minutes or until edges are lightly browned. Bake larger cookies 10-12 minutes or until edges are lightly browned. If you prefer crunchier cookies, bake for 2-3 minutes longer, or until entire cookie is a light golden color.

**Variation:**
For those who don't want a cinnamon/sugar cookie, roll each cookie in plain sugar. Add chocolate or rainbow sprinkles on top of each cookie prior to baking.

# Almond or Almond Chocolate-Chip Cookies

*This is an excellent recipe. If your taste buds like the combination of almond and chocolate, here is a wonderful cookie for these two flavors. Little children enjoy making faces and hair out of the almonds and chocolate chips prior to baking the cookies.*

**36 plus small or 8-9 large cookies**

Preheat oven to 350 degrees F.

½ cup plus 1 tablespoon sugar, set aside.

1 cup (2 sticks) butter
1 cup sugar
1 teaspoon vanilla
1 teaspoon almond extract
1 egg
2 cups plus 1 tablespoon flour
1 teaspoon baking powder
¼ teaspoon baking soda
⅛ teaspoon cream of tarter
½ cup sliced almonds for the top of each cookie
½ cup chocolate chips for the top of each cookie (optional) or
   ⅔ cup mini chips for smaller Almond Chocolate-Chip Cookies

1. Cream together the butter, sugar and vanilla.
2. Add the remaining ingredients, ending with the egg. Mix all the ingredients together, except for large chocolate chips and almonds, for 2 minutes on medium-high in an electric mixer. (If baking small Almond Chocolate-Chip Cookies, add the mini chips after adding the egg and mix thoroughly.)

*continued on next page*

3. Grease 2 cookies sheets.

4. For smaller cookies, roll 1 tablespoon of dough into a ball with the palms of your hands. For larger cookies (4-5 inches), roll ⅓ cup of dough into a ball with the palms of your hands.

5. Roll each cookie in the sugar and completely coat, and place on prepared cookie sheets.

6. Slightly flatten each cookie with the palm of your hand. Sprinkle the top of each cookie with almond slices and chocolate chips (if using chips).

7. Bake smaller cookies 7-10 minutes or until edges are light brown. Bake larger cookies 10-12 minutes or until the edges are light brown.

# Chocolate Chocolate-Chip Cookies

*This cookie reminds me of a flattened-out brownie. I knew that I definitely had a winner when I first came up with this recipe. These have been referred to as a "chocolate lover's taste of heaven." The choice of what to add to these cookies (chips, nuts or dried fruit) is up to you.*

**40 plus small or 10-12 large cookies**

Preheat oven to 375 degrees F.

1 cup butter
1 cup brown sugar
¾ sugar
1 tablespoon vanilla
⅔ cup cocoa
3 eggs
1 teaspoon baking soda
2½ cups minus 1 tablespoon flour
1½ cups chocolate chips
Additions if desired: 1 cup macadamia nuts, walnuts, pecans, peanuts, peanut butter chips, white chocolate chips or dried fruit

1. Cream together the butter, sugars and vanilla.

2. Add the cocoa to the butter mixture and mix thoroughly. Add the remaining ingredients and mix together thoroughly.

3. Grease 2 cookie sheets.

4. For smaller cookies, drop a tablespoonful of dough onto prepared cookie sheets. For larger cookies (4-5 inches), place ⅓ cup dough onto prepared cookie sheets. Slightly flatten each large cookie with the palm of your hand.

5. Bake smaller cookies 7-10 minutes or until edges are brown. Bake larger cookies 10-13 minutes or until the edges are brown.

# Real Scottish Shortbread

**The following recipes can be divided in half if a smaller amount is preferred.**

*The next three recipes are exquisite. The base recipe came to me directly from a Grandmother, whom, I was told, has always lived in the same town in Scotland. It is the real stuff! Each cookie just melts in your mouth. The old secret to real shortbread is that the cookie dough is rolled out on plain old granulated sugar; nothing else will do. For over a decade, I have used these recipes as my basic Christmas cookies. I think that this recipe is perfect for cutout cookies, especially cinnamon bears, my favorite.*

**Amount depends on size of cookie, average 36 plus, 2-inch cookies**

Preheat oven to 325 degrees F.

1 pound or 2 cups (4 sticks) butter (no substitutions)
1 cup powdered sugar
4 cups plus 1 tablespoon flour

1. Mix together the butter, sugar and flour until completely mixed and until there are no crumbs remaining in the bottom of bowl.

2. Grease 3 cookie sheets.

3. Sprinkle entire surface of a cutting board or countertop with sugar, cinnamon sugar or colored sugar. **Do not use flour or powdered sugar.**

4. Roll out one-third of the dough on sugar, cinnamon sugar or colored sugar.

5. Cut out cookies with cookie cutters and place onto the prepared cookie sheets. Gather up the leftover dough and add it to another portion of the remaining dough. Sprinkle and spread more sugar onto the rolling surface and repeat rolling and cutting out cookies until all the dough is gone.

6. Bake 4-5 minutes (depending on the size) or until slightly brown around the edges.

Allow cookies to cool 10-15 minutes before tasting; if cookies are handled too soon, they will fall apart.

# Real Scottish Shortbread Sandwiches

*These are scrumptious—absolutely perfect for afternoon tea. For a special someone, use a heart-shaped, 2-inch cookie cutter and present the shortbread wrapped in colored cellophane on Valentine's Day.*

**15-20, 2-inch sandwich cookies**

Preheat oven to 325 degrees F.

½ to ⅔ cup of jam
Set jam aside.

1 pound or 2 cups (4 sticks) butter (no substitutions)
1 cup powdered sugar
4 cups plus 1 tablespoon flour

1. Mix together the butter, sugar and flour until and no crumbs are left in the bottom of the bowl.

2. Grease 2-3 cookie sheets.

3. Sprinkle entire surface of a cutting board or countertop with sugar or colored sugar. **Do not use flour or powdered sugar.**

4. Roll out half the dough onto sugar or colored sugar. Use a cookie cutter that is evenly shaped, such as a circle, heart, star or diamond. Do not use a cookie cutter larger then 2½ inches as the dough will break. Cut out cookies and place onto prepared cookie sheets.

5. Depending on size of cookie, spread 1-1½ teaspoons of jam in the center of each cookie.

6. Top each cookie with a same-shape cookie.

7. Repeat rolling and cutting out dough with the remaining dough, spreading a little jam and remembering to always sprinkle a bit more sugar onto the rolling surface prior to rolling out more dough.

8. Bake 10-15 minutes or until the edges are lightly brown.

# Lemon Shortbread

*If you like shortbread, and you like the zest of lemon, then you'll like this recipe. These are great with afternoon tea or as a special treat any time of the day.*

**Amount depends on size of cookie, average 36 plus, 2-inch cookies**

Preheat oven to 325 degrees F.

1 pound or 2 cups (4 sticks) butter (no substitutions)
1 cup powdered sugar
4 cups plus 1 ½ tablespoons flour
1 teaspoon lemon extract or 1 tablespoon fresh squeezed lemon juice
2 teaspoons lemon curd

1. Mix together the butter, sugar, flour, lemon juice and lemon curd until completely mixed and there are no crumbs remain in the bottom of the bowl.

2. Grease 2-3 cookie sheets

3. Sprinkle entire surface of a cutting board or countertop with sugar or colored sugar.
   **Do not use flour or powdered sugar.**

4. Roll out one-third of dough on sugar or colored sugar; cut out cookies with cookie cutters and place onto prepared cookie sheets. Gather up the leftover dough and add it to another portion of the remaining dough. Sprinkle and spread more sugar onto the rolling surface and repeat rolling and cutting out cookies until all the dough is gone.

5. Bake 4-5 minutes (depending on the size) or until slightly brown around the edges.

# Lemon Snickerdoodles

*This recipe is just as good as the other Snickerdoodles recipe (on page 11), except a hint of lemon is added to it. If you like lemon cookies, then you're sure to enjoy these.*

**30 plus small or 8-10 large cookies**

Preheat oven to 350 degrees F.

¾ cup additional sugar, set aside.

1 cup butter
1 cup sugar
1 tablespoon lemon curd
2 teaspoons real or freshly squeezed lemon juice
1 egg
2 cups plus 2 tablespoons of flour
¼ teaspoon baking soda
1 teaspoon baking powder
⅛ teaspoon cream of tartar

1. Cream together the butter, sugar, lemon curd and juice. Add the remaining ingredients and mix together thoroughly.

2. Grease 2 cookie sheets.

3. For smaller cookies, roll 1 tablespoon of dough into a ball in the palms of your hands. For larger cookies, roll a ⅓ cup of dough into a ball in the palms of your hands.

4. Roll each ball into additional sugar, place on a prepared cookie sheet and slightly flatten with the palm of your hand.

5. Bake smaller cookies 7-10 minutes or until golden around the edges. Bake larger cookies 10-14 minutes or until golden around the edges.

# Grandmom's Sugar Cookies

*I grew up on this recipe; whenever I make these cookies I am reminded of the scents in the hallway of my Grandmom's apartment building and the joy of eating them as a little girl. This recipe can make my mouth water as soon as I smell them, just before they are ready to come out of the oven.*

**36 plus, 2-inch cookies**

1 cup (2 sticks) butter
1 cup sugar
1 tablespoon vanilla
2 eggs
3¾ cups plus 2 tablespoons flour
2 teaspoons baking powder
¼ cup plus 1 tablespoon heavy cream
Colored sugar, decorative sugar shapes or cinnamon sugar to use for the topping

1. Cream together the butter, sugar and vanilla. Add the remaining ingredients and mix thoroughly.

2. Divide the dough in half.

3. Wrap each half of the dough in cellophane and refrigerate for 3 hours.

4. Preheat oven to 350 degrees F.

5. Grease 2 cookie sheets.

6. While dough is cool, roll half the dough out onto a lightly floured surface. With cookie cutters, cut the dough out into desired shapes. Place each cookie onto a prepared cookie sheet. Gather up the remaining dough and repeat until all the dough is used.

7. Decorate each cookie with colored sugar, decorative shapes, sprinkles or cinnamon sugar.

8. Bake 10-14 minutes or until the edges are light brown.

# Grandmom's Chocolate Sugar Cookies

*This is a wonderful Sugar Cookie for chocolate lovers.*

**30 plus cookies**

½ cup additional sugar, set aside.

3 squares of unsweetened chocolate, plus
1 heaping tablespoon of mini or regular sized semisweet chocolate chips
1 cup (2 sticks) margarine
1 cup sugar
1 large egg
2 teaspoons vanilla
2 cups plus 2 tablespoons flour
1 teaspoon baking soda
Pinch of salt for extra flavor (optional)

1. Melt the unsweetened chocolate, chocolate chips and margarine together.

2. Cream together the sugar, egg and vanilla.

3. Add the melted chocolate and margarine to the sugar mixture and mix together. Add the flour and baking soda to the chocolate mixture. Mix all the ingredients together thoroughly.

4. Cover and refrigerate the dough for 30 minutes.

5. Preheat oven to 375 degrees F.

6. Grease 2 cookie sheets.

7. Roll 1½ tablespoons of dough between the palms of your hands to make balls. Roll each ball into the additional sugar.

*continued on next page*

8. Place each cookie onto a prepared cookie sheet. Slightly flatten each cookie with the palm of your hand or use a fork to make a crisscross design.

9. Bake 8-10 minutes.

**Variation:**
See the Jam-Filled Chocolate Cookies recipe on the next page.

# Jam-Filled Chocolate Cookies

---

*A delicious alternative to the Chocolate Sugar Cookies.*

½ cup jam

1. Follow the for the Chocolate Sugar Cookies on page 21.

2. Indent your thumb into each cookie ball after rolling it in additional sugar.

3. Fill the center with 1 teaspoon of your favorite jam; do not flatten jam-filled cookies.

4. Bake 8-10 minutes.

# Libby's Favorite Low-Fat Applesauce Cookies

*Libby was a favorite private customer of mine who was unable to digest butter well, so she preferred canola or safflower oil. For this reason, and because I wanted a cookie that was low in cholesterol, I came up with this recipe. These cookies are fantastic for all to enjoy, particularly for those with a special diet to follow.*

**30 plus cookies**

Preheat oven to 350 degrees F.

½ cup canola or safflower oil
1⅓ cups brown sugar or 1¼ cups Twin brown sugar substitute
1½ cups chunky applesauce or sugarless chunky applesauce
2 eggs or equivalent amount of liquid egg substitute
2½ cups flour
1 teaspoon baking soda
1 tablespoon cinnamon
½ teaspoon each nutmeg and cloves
Additions if desired: raisins, chopped nuts, or as Libby preferred, dried cranberries

1. Mix together the oil, sugar and applesauce.

2. Add the remaining ingredients, and mix all the ingredients together thoroughly.

3. Grease 2 cookie sheets.

4. Drop dough by a tablespoonful or with a small ice cream scoop onto prepared cookie sheets. For larger cookies, drop ⅓ cup dough onto prepared cookie sheets. Flatten each large cookie slightly with the palm of your hand.

5. Bake smaller cookies 7-10 minutes or until lightly browned around the edges. Bake larger cookies 9-13 minutes or until lightly brown around the edges.

# Spritz Cookies

*When I first came up with this recipe, it took no time to determine that these cookies will always be a favorite of mine. They are so good that they do not need a lot of sugar on top—just a tad for decoration. I have seen small children light up like sunshine when they saw their favorite rainbow sprinkle cookies freshly baked in a pastry case.*

**30 plus cookies**

Preheat oven to 375 degrees F.

1 cup butter
¾ cup sugar
1 egg yolk
1 tablespoon vanilla
2 cups plus 2 tablespoons flour
For topping, use either red or green colored cherries, sugar dots, colored sugars, sprinkles, etc.

1. Mix together all the ingredients on medium-high for 3-4 minutes or until dough gathers and is completely blended together.

2. Grease 2 cookie sheets

3. Gather 1 tablespoonful of dough together, and roll into a ball in the palms of your hands. Place balls onto the prepared cookie sheets.

4. With a fork, make a crisscross pattern on top of each cookie. Sprinkle each cookie with your choice of toppings or place ½ a candied cherry on the center of cookie.

5. Bake 5-7 minutes or until the edges are barely brown.

**Variation:**
See the recipe on the next page.

# Spritz Thumbprint Cookies

½-⅔ cup of jam
2-3 tablespoons powdered sugar

1. Follow the recipe for the Spritz Cookies on page 25.

2. Roll 1½ tablespoons of dough into a ball with the palms of your hands.

3. Press thumb in center, and fill impression with a teaspoon of jam.

4. Bake for 5-7 minutes or until barely brown.

5. After baking the thumbprint cookies, sprinkle each lightly with powdered sugar.

# Grandmom's Thumbprint Cookies

*This recipe is another of my favorites made by my Grandmom. I am particularly fond of the cookies when made with the raisin filling, although it does not matter which filling you use. Choose a personal filling preference or make a few of each. You will probably eat too many anyway, they're so good.*

**24 plus cookies**

Preheat oven to 375 degrees F.

NUT AND/OR RAISIN FILLING:
2 tablespoons sugar
¼ cup butter, melted
1 cup chopped nuts and/or raisins
1 teaspoon cinnamon
Mix together and set aside.
Substitute the above filling for ⅔ cup jam

1 cup butter (no substitutions)
1 cup sugar
A few drops of vanilla
2½ cups plus 1 tablespoon flour
3 hard-boiled egg yolks

1. Cream together the butter, sugar and vanilla.

2. Add the flour and egg yolks to the butter mixture, and mix all the ingredients together thoroughly. If dough appears too dry, add 1 teaspoon milk at a time to the dough. Do not exceed 1 tablespoon milk.

3. Grease cookie sheets.

4. Gather 1 tablespoon of dough together and roll into a ball between the palms of your hands.

5. Press your thumb into each ball. Fill the impression with a teaspoon of jam, nut and/or raisin filling.

6. Bake 10-12 minutes or until lightly brown on the edges.

# Grandmom's Pinwheel Cookies

---

*My Grandmom would only bake this recipe once in a blue moon, but when she did, the cookies never lasted long. If you like the pairing of chocolate and vanilla, then you are sure to enjoy these cookies.*

**24 plus cookies**

1 square of unsweetened chocolate
½ cup (1 stick) butter
¾ cup sugar
2 eggs
1 tablespoon vanilla
1¼ cups flour
¼ teaspoon baking powder
1 cup chocolate sprinkles, set aside

1. Melt the square of unsweetened chocolate over hot water or in the microwave and set aside.

2. Cream together the butter, sugar, eggs and vanilla. Add the flour and baking powder to the butter mixture. Mix all the ingredients together thoroughly.

3. On a floured piece of waxed paper, roll half of the dough until rectangular in shape and ¼-inch thick.

4. Add to the remaining dough, the melted square of unsweetened chocolate. Mix the chocolate thoroughly into the dough.

5. On a separate piece of waxed paper, lightly flour and roll the chocolate dough into the same size and shape as the vanilla dough.

6. Invert chocolate dough onto the top of the vanilla dough. Roll the stacked pieces of dough out as much as you can, but no less than ⅛-inch thick. Remove the top layer of waxed paper.

7. Use the bottom piece of waxed paper to guide you in rolling the dough up like a tight jellyroll or cookie roll.

8. Sprinkle the chocolate sprinkles onto a third piece of waxed paper, and gently lift the cookie roll, place it on top of the chocolate sprinkles and roll in the sprinkles to coat all sides of the cookie roll.

9. Wrap the cookie roll in waxed paper. Refrigerate 2-3 hours.

10. Let dough stand at room temperature 30 minutes.

11. Preheat oven to 350 degrees F.

12. Grease 2 cookie sheets.

13. Slice cookies about ½-inch thick and place on the prepared cookie sheets.

14. Bake 5-7 minutes or until the edges are lightly browned.

# Low-Fat Gingersnaps

*This recipe is too darn good to be lower in fat, but it is. Although, these cookies are softer, they are just as spicy and good as a crunchy snap. Libby, a great customer of mine, would always request that I bake her two batches of this recipe. She wouldn't let them go bad either—she would freeze them and take some out as needed. She says these cookies last about a month in the freezer without losing their flavor.*

**30 plus cookies**

Preheat oven to 325 degrees F.

¾ cup sugar
2 tablespoons cinnamon
Mix together and set aside in a small bowl.

½ cup (1 stick) margarine
½ cup canola or safflower oil
1 cup sugar
½ cup plus 1 teaspoon brown sugar
2 eggs or equivalent amount of liquid egg substitute
⅓ cup molasses
2½ cups flour
2 teaspoons baking soda
2 teaspoons ginger
½ teaspoon nutmeg
½ teaspoon cloves
2 teaspoons cinnamon
Additions if desired: raisins and/or dried cranberries, nuts, etc.

1. Mix together the margarine, oil and sugars.

2. Add the eggs and the molasses to the sugar mixture, and mix thoroughly.

3. Add the flour, baking soda, spices and choice of an addition to the mixture. Mix all the ingredients together thoroughly. This batter will be very moist.

4. Grease 2 cookie sheets

5. Lightly flour the palms of your hands (optional).

6. Use a tablespoon full of batter or use a small ice cream scoop to gather the dough, and roll the dough into a ball with the palms of your floured hands.

7. Roll each cookie ball in the cinnamon sugar mixture, place onto the prepared cookie sheets and lightly flatten each cookie with the palm of your hand.

8. Bake 10-14 minutes, depending upon whether you want soft or crunchy cookies.

# Nut Cookies

*For those who like nuts and a good dunking cookie, this is a recipe for you. Personally, I think they go splendidly with hot apple cider or a glass of warm brandy on a cold winter day. I have been told that these cookies are a wonderful complement to coffee or tea at first light of morning.*

**40 plus cookies**

1 cup (2 sticks) butter or margarine
2 cups brown sugar
1 egg
1 tablespoon vanilla
3⅔ cups flour
1 teaspoon baking soda
1 cup finely chopped pecans or walnuts

1. Cream together the butter, sugar, egg and vanilla.

2. Sift together flour and baking soda. Add sifted flour to butter mixture and mix thoroughly.

3. Divide dough in half.

4. Roll each half into a 1½-inch thick log or cookie roll.

5. On a piece of waxed paper, sprinkle the chopped nuts.

6. Roll each log/cookie roll into the nuts to coat, and then wrap each log in cellophane and refrigerate for 1½-2 hours.

7. Preheat oven to 375 degrees F.

8. Grease 2-3 cookie sheets.

9. Slice each roll into ¼-inch slices.

10. Bake 8-10 minutes or until golden around the edges.

# Pecan Balls

*I make this recipe every year for Christmas. Rich and delicate, these cookies look astounding and quite tempting on a Christmas dessert table or in a gift basket. When your temptation gets the best of you, these cookies will simply melt in your mouth.*

**40 plus cookies**

Preheat oven to 300 degrees F.

1 cup (2 sticks) butter (no substitutions)
¼ cup sugar
Scant 2 cups flour
2 teaspoons vanilla
2 cups finely ground pecan nutmeats (or walnuts or hazelnuts)
 (To grind the nuts into nutmeats, pour whole or chopped nuts into a food processor and grind them until you have 2 cups full. Or, place whole or chopped nuts into a plastic baggie and with a rolling pin beat them until they become ground enough to fill 2 measuring cups with the nutmeats.)
½ cup powdered sugar and/or cocoa

1. Cream together the butter and sugar.

2. Add the flour and vanilla to the butter mixture. Mix the dough thoroughly; it will be just a bit dry.

3. Grease 2-3 cookie sheets

4. Roll 1 tablespoonful of dough into a ball in the palms of your hands.

5. Roll each ball in the nutmeats to completely coat. Place each ball onto the prepared cookie sheets, making sure the balls do not touch each other.

6. Bake 25-30 minutes or until they begin to turn golden.

7. Immediately upon removal from the oven, roll each ball into a bowl full of powdered sugar and/or cocoa.

*continued on next page*

**Variation:**
For an extra special treat, prior to forming dough into balls, place a semisweet chocolate chip into the center of the dough and then roll the dough into balls.

# Miniature Cinnamon Swirl Cookies

*My customers and friends say these are the best "dunkers" I've ever made. Obviously, these cookies are perfect served with coffee or tea. Your friends and family will think you spent hours on these extravagant treats, when in reality, they do not take too long to make at all.*

**25 plus cookies**

Preheat oven to 375 degrees F.

⅔ cup sugar
2 tablespoons cinnamon
Mix cinnamon and sugar together and set aside in a separate bowl.

¼ cup (½ stick) butter
Melt and set aside.

⅔ cup (1 ⅓ sticks) melted butter or margarine
⅓ cup sugar
3 cups plus 2 tablespoons flour
1 ¼ teaspoons baking powder
1 cup plus 1 tablespoon milk
½ cup raisins and/or chopped walnuts, set aside
2 teaspoons molasses

1. Mix together the ⅔ cup of butter or margarine, sugar, flour and baking powder while gradually adding the milk. Mix all the ingredients together thoroughly.

2. When the dough begins to gather together in the mixing bowl, take it out of the bowl and place the dough on a floured surface; knead 10-12 times.

*continued on next page*

3. Divide the dough in half. With your hands, flatten and gently stretch the dough prior to rolling. Roll each half of dough into about a 20x12-inch square (the size does not need to be exact).

4. With a pastry brush or butter knife, distribute half of the melted ¼ cup of butter all over dough. Sprinkle half the cinnamon sugar all over dough. Lightly trickle 1 teaspoon of molasses all over the dough, making sure that there are no clumps of molasses. Sprinkle half the dough with raisins and/or chopped walnuts (optional).

5. Roll up from the long side of the dough into a long, tight jellyroll or cookie roll.

6. Grease 2 cookie sheets.

7. Slice the cookie roll into 1-inch pieces. Place each cookie onto prepared cookie sheets and lightly flatten with the palm of your hand. Sprinkle each cookie with a pinch of additional cinnamon sugar.

8. Repeat with the remaining dough.

9. Bake approximately 15 minutes or until the edges begin to turn golden.

# Lebkuchen

---

*This is a time-consuming recipe. Be patient—it is well worth the effort. This recipe belonged to the Grandmother of a friend of mine. My friend was kind enough to share it with me and now I'm sharing it with you. This recipe is a Christmastime delicacy, to be shared year after year with family, friends and a warm beverage.*

**36-48 cookies depending on the size of the slices**

Preheat oven to 350 degrees F.

3 eggs
4 cups brown sugar
1 cup Crisco
4 cups light molasses
1¼ teaspoon salt
Pinch of pepper
2 tablespoons anise seed
2 teaspoons cinnamon
1 level teaspoon nutmeg
1 level teaspoon cloves
16 cups flour
1 teaspoon baking soda
1 cup sour milk (1 tablespoon vinegar plus cup of milk)
1 pound blanched almonds, finely chopped

1. Beat the eggs, add the sugar and continue beating. Beat in the Crisco.
2. Add the molasses, spices and then the flour and baking soda alternately with the milk to the egg mixture. Use a mixer until the dough is too stiff to beat, and then work the dough by hand until all ingredients are thoroughly incorporated.

*continued on next page*

3. Lightly spray a cookie sheet with pan spray.

4. Push and spread batter to completely cover the cookie sheet. You may need to patch uncovered sections with extra dough. Press edges square with a knife.

5. Cover the dough with almonds and lightly press them into the dough.

6. Bake 20 minutes.

7. Remove the cookie sheet from the oven and immediately cut the cookies into 3x5-inch squares and then cut each square in half.

8. Gently remove the squares from the pan after 5-6 minutes. Place each square onto waxed paper and allow it to cool completely prior to adding the glaze.

GLAZE:
1. Boil 2 cups sugar and 1½ cups water until combination boils and spins. Stir well.
2. Pour over squares, allow to cool and **enjoy!**

# Cinnamon Nut and/or Raisin Cookies

*I came up with this recipe one cold winter day when I turned on the oven just for heat
and I wanted the house to smell like cinnamon. They turned out pleasantly tasteful.*

**30 plus cookies**

Preheat oven to 350 degrees F.

1 cup butter
¾ cup brown sugar
¾ cup sugar
2 eggs
1 tablespoon vanilla
2 tablespoons molasses
2⅔ cups flour
1 teaspoon baking soda
2 teaspoons cinnamon
1⅓ cups chopped walnuts and/or pecans, and/or raisins

1. Cream together the butter, sugars, eggs and vanilla. Add the remaining ingredients to the butter mixture. Mix all the ingredients together thoroughly.

2. Grease 2 cookie sheets

3. For smaller cookies, drop 1 tablespoonful or a small ice cream scoop full of dough onto the prepared cookie sheets. For larger cookies, use ⅓ cup full of dough. Lightly flatten each large cookie with the palm of your hand.

4. Bake smaller cookies 7-10 minutes and bake larger cookies 10-14 minutes, depending on whether you prefer your cookies soft or crunchy.

# Kisses and Cherries

---

*My favorite fruit happens to be cherries, so of course, I had to come up with a good cherry cookie recipe. I tasted cherry-chocolate store-bought cookies at a party and immediately thought I could develop a similar recipe. I played a little, got some tips from my Aunt Lil, and what a fine surprise when they came out of the oven after the fifth try.*

**30 plus cookies**

Preheat oven to 325 degrees F.

1 cup (2 sticks) butter
1 cup powdered sugar
3 teaspoons maraschino cherry juice
1 ½ teaspoons vanilla
¼ teaspoon almond extract (optional)
2 ⅓ cups of flour
A healthy ½ cup chopped maraschino cherries
⅔ cup mini chocolate chips
   or ¾ bag Hershey Kisses, unwrapped and set aside
¼ cup sugar, set aside

1. Cream together the butter, sugar, juice, vanilla and almond extract. Add the flour alternately with the cherries to the butter mixture and continue mixing. If using mini chocolate chips, add them with the cherries.

2. Grease 2 cookie sheets.

3. Roll 1 ½ tablespoons dough into a ball for each cookie.

4. Slightly flatten the balls with a smooth-bottom glass coated with sugar. (Green colored sugar looks great on these cookies at Christmastime. To keep sugar on the glass bottom, dampen it with a wet cloth and constantly dip it into the sugar.)

5. Bake 13-15 minutes or until the bottoms are lightly browned.

6. If using Hershey Kisses instead of mini chips, immediately after removing the cookie sheets from the oven, place 1 kiss into the center of each cookie, and let cool for about 10-15 minutes before removing from the pan.

# Grandmom's Rugelach

*When asked what my favorite cookie is, I always mention this one. These cookies will always bring up memories of growing up and visits with my Grandmom. I know of many customers who just can't get enough of these cookies and continue to ask me to make them up a batch. These cookies freeze beautifully, so make a few batches and then you can eat them whenever you want without all the fuss.*

**40 plus cookies**

¾ cup sugar or sugar substitute
2 tablespoons cinnamon
Mix the sugar and cinnamon together and set aside.

½ cup additional butter, set aside.

Scant 1 cup jam or sugar-free jam, set aside. (I think apricot or raspberry work best, but any flavor works well.)

1 cup (2 sticks) butter
7 ounces cream cheese
3¼ cups flour
1 cup raisins and/or walnuts or mini chocolate chips
2 teaspoons of molasses (do not use if making sugar-free)

1. Mix together the 1 cup of butter with the cream cheese and the flour.

2. Divide the dough in half, roll each half into a ball, flatten each ball slightly and wrap in cellophane. Refrigerate each ball of dough 30 minutes or longer.

3. Preheat oven to 375 degrees F.

4. Roll out 1 ball of the dough onto a lightly floured surface until circular and about 12-14 inches around.

5. Spread half the additional butter lightly around the entire circle. Spread half the jam all over the circle. Leaving about a ¼ inch from the edge of the dough empty, spread half the raisins, nuts and/or chips around the dough. Sprinkle entire circle generously with one-third of the cinnamon sugar. Drizzle 1 teaspoon of molasses all over the cinnamon sugar, making sure there are no clumps of the molasses.

6. Grease 2 cookie sheets.

7. Cut the prepared dough circle into 10-12 triangular sections. Do not separate sections.

8. Roll each section up tightly like a croissant, starting at the outer edge. Pinch the final point slightly so it sticks to the dough.

9. Repeat this process with the remaining dough.

10. Place each cookie onto the prepared cookie sheets.

11. Mix together:
    1 egg yolk
    2 tablespoons water

12. With a pastry brush or fork, brush each cookie with the egg yolk/water mixture. Sprinkle the last ⅓ cup of cinnamon sugar onto the cookies.

13. Bake 14-16 minutes or until golden brown. The cookies should be a bit crunchy on top, but softer in the middle.

# Schnecken

*I am not sure who in my family created this recipe. I remember devouring these cookies as a kid, but didn't know where the recipe came from since it was not in my Grandmom's Tin Box. One day, while visiting my parents in Philadelphia, I found it written down in my Mother's cooking notebook. I proceeded to take the recipe home to Colorado. I made some adjustments for High Altitude baking, and when they came out of the oven, these cookies tasted just as I had remembered. This recipe is similar to my Grandmom's Rugalach, but much easier to make.*

**36 plus cookies**

Preheat oven to 375 degrees F.

¾ cup sugar or sugar substitute
¼ cup cinnamon (less if you like)
Mix the cinnamon and sugar together and set aside.

½ cup (1 stick) butter, melted and set aside.

½ cup (1 stick) butter
2 tablespoons sugar or sugar substitute
2 cups plus 2 tablespoons flour
1 tablespoon baking powder
1 egg plus enough milk to make ½ cup (add 1 extra teaspoon milk at a time if dough is very dry, do not exceed 1 tablespoon)
1½ cups raisins and/or chopped walnuts

1. Mix ½ cup butter, sugar, flour and baking powder by hand or with a slow mixer until fully incorporated.

2. Knead dough for about 4-5 minutes on a floured surface.

3. Divide the dough in half.

4. Roll each half of the dough on a floured board until thin, but not too thin.

5. With a pastry brush or fork, brush half the melted butter onto dough. Sprinkle half the cinnamon sugar mixture all over the dough. Sprinkle half the raisins and/or nuts on top of the cinnamon sugar.

6. Roll the dough up tightly into a jellyroll or cookie roll.

7. Pinch the seam of the cookie rolls into the cookie base to seal the roll.

8. Repeat with the remaining dough.

9. Grease 2 cookie sheets.

10. Slice each roll into 1½-inch pieces.

11. Place each cookie onto the prepared cookie sheets. Sprinkle a pinch of cinnamon sugar on top of each cookie.

12. Bake about 15 minutes or until firm and golden brown around the edges.

# Mom's Cream Cheese Cookies

*My Mother always told everyone she only baked from scratch. Ha!
One day, while skipping school, I found a Duncan Hines Brownie box in the trash can. Boy did she and I laugh as I teased her about my find! I always thought the following recipe was made from scratch, until I found it in her cooking notebook after she passed away.*

**36 plus cookies**

Preheat oven to 375 degrees F.

¼ cup (½ stick) butter or margarine
8 ounces cream cheese
1 egg yolk
2 teaspoons vanilla
1 box yellow cake mix
Colored sugars or sprinkles

1. Cream together the butter and cream cheese. Add the egg yolk and vanilla to the butter and cream cheese and continue mixing together.

2. Add the cake mix in 3 parts, making sure to completely mix each portion into the creamed mixture prior to adding the next portion.

3. Refrigerate dough 15-30 minutes.

4. Grease 2 cookie sheets.

5. Drop the dough by a teaspoonful for each cookie onto prepared cookie sheets.

6. Decorate with colored sugar or sprinkles.

7. Bake 7-9 minutes or until the edges begin to brown.

# Sour Cream Cookies

*I can only assume that my Grandmom used to read a lot of recipes in the newspaper and magazines, for I continue to find recipe clippings in her treasured Tin Box. Obviously, she only saved recipes after she tried them and found them to her liking, or that wonderful Tin Box would be too full to close. The following recipe comes from an old piece of newspaper titled "The Evening Bulletin, Philadelphia, Thursday, September 30, 1948". I remember my Father telling me that she sent these cookies to him when he was in the Korean War. They are still as good today as they were back then.*

**36 plus cookies**

½ cup (1 stick) butter
1 cup sugar
3½ cups flour
¼ teaspoon baking soda
½ teaspoon nutmeg
½ teaspoon cinnamon
½ cup sour cream
Almonds, jam or maraschino cherry halves for the top of each cookie

1. Cream together the butter and sugar.

2. Add the flour, baking soda and spices alternately with the sour cream to the butter mixture.

3. Mix thoroughly and refrigerate 1 hour.

4. Preheat oven to 350 degrees F.

5. Grease 2 cookie sheets.

6. Handling a small amount of dough at a time, roll the dough onto a floured surface until ¼-inch thick.

7. With cookie cutters, cut the dough into shapes, though not too large, and place cookies on the prepared cookie sheets.

8. Top each cookie with sliced almonds, 1 teaspoon of jam or a maraschino cherry half.

9. Bake 8-10 minutes or until the edges begin to brown.

# Thoughts for a Good Friend

May the light always find you on a dreary day.

When you need to be home, may you find your way.

May you always find courage to take a chance.

And never find frogs in your underpants.

*Anonymous*

# Cakes

---

* All recipes can be doubled or tripled.
* Use only soft, or at room temperature butter, margarine or cream cheese.
* Cakes will dry out quickly at high altitude, so keep them covered with a lid or cellophane
(unless specified otherwise) at all times when not serving.
* All these cakes can be frozen for up to eight days.

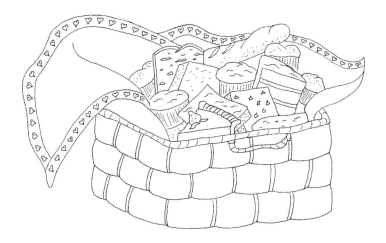

**Clockwise from top:** Chocolate Cream Cheese, Honey Apple, Great Grandmother's Cinnamon Streusel, Carol's Favorite Lemon Cake

# Happiness Cake

*A friend gave this recipe to me many, many years ago. It is one of the finest cakes I have ever made. I hope this recipe will be shared by many generations to come.*

Preheat oven to 98.6 degrees F.

Mix thoroughly:
1 cup good thoughts
1 cup kind deeds
1 cup well-beaten faults
1 cup consideration for others
2 cups sacrifice
3 plus cups forgiveness

Add:
Tears of joy, sorrow and sympathy
Flavor with love and kindly service
Fold in 4 cups prayer and faith
Blend well
Fold into daily life
Bake well with the warmth of human kindness
and serve with a smile any time
It will satisfy the hunger of starved souls.

# Great Grandmother's Cinnamon Streusel Cake

*If you like streusel cakes, this is for you. The recipe has been a favorite among friends and family for more than 100 years. To my knowledge, there have been no complaints—only requests. This recipe has also been one of my top best sellers for the past 12 years of baking professionally. My mechanic, Bruce, says this recipe is "absolutely awesome" and has yet to ever turn down a piece.*

Preheat oven to 350 degrees F.

TOPPING AND FILLING:
2½ cups packed brown sugar
½ cup (1 stick) butter
⅓ cup cinnamon
Mix these 3 ingredients together to make the streusel, and set aside in a separate bowl.

CAKE:
1 cup (2 sticks) butter
1⅓ cups sugar
6 eggs
3 cups plus 2 tablespoons flour
2 teaspoons baking powder
2 teaspoons baking soda
2 cups sour cream or plain yogurt (if you don't like sour cream)

1. Cream together the butter, sugar and eggs. Add the flour, baking powder and baking soda to the butter mixture. Mix the batter thoroughly.

2. Grease a 9x13-inch pan or 10x2-inch round pan and lightly flour the bottom and sides (if you are going to remove the cake from the pan).

3. Spread half the batter into the pan. Sprinkle half the streusel all over the bottom layer of batter.

4. Repeat with the remaining ingredients, batter and then streusel on top.

5. Bake approximately 45-55 minutes or until an inserted knife or toothpick comes out clean. Let cool an hour for best flavor.

# Raspberry Cream Cheese Cake

*Friends and customers have always enjoyed this recipe. It combines two particularly favored flavors: raspberry and cream cheese. The result: a light, pleasing texture and taste. If your palate is enticed by raspberries and chocolate, then please, add chocolate after baking for a different delight. Often, I received requests to bake this cake for a birthday cake.*

Preheat oven to 350 degrees F.

¾ cup (1½ sticks) butter or margarine
12 ounces cream cheese
1½ cups sugar
1 tablespoon vanilla
3¼ cups flour
3 eggs
⅓ cup whole milk
1½ teaspoons baking powder
¾ teaspoon baking soda
¾ cup raspberry jam, set aside
Scant 2 cups chocolate chips (optional)

1. Cream together the butter, cream cheese, sugar and vanilla.

2. Mix half the flour and all the eggs into the butter mixture.

3. Mix thoroughly and add the remaining flour. Trust me—add the flour as described. Continue mixing until all the flour is fully incorporated into the batter.

4. Grease and lightly flour the bottom and sides of a 9x13-inch pan or a bundt pan.

5. Spread half the batter evenly around the chosen pan.

6. Dollop tablespoonsful from half the jam, all over the batter.

7. Repeat with the remaining batter and jam.

8. Swirl the jam around in the batter with a butter knife. **Do not mix! Swirl!**

9. Bake 40-45 minutes or until an inserted knife comes out clean. Let cool prior to serving.

If you want to add the chocolate chips, do so immediately after the cake is removed from the oven. Sprinkle the chocolate chips all over the top of the cake, wait 5 minutes and proceed to gently spread melted chips to cover the surface of the cake. Let cake cool 15 minutes prior to covering with cellophane or a cake lid.

**Variation:**
Strawberry jam can be used as a substitute for the raspberry jam.

# Carol's Favorite Lemon Cake

*I call this incredible treat "Carol's Favorite." Carol is a dear friend of mine, and this recipe just happens to be her favorite cake that I bake. Some of you may remember an old folk song called "The Lemon Tree." "Lemon tree very pretty and the lemon flower is sweet, but the taste of the poor lemon, is impossible to eat." The chorus of that song is appropriate to explain the sweet/sour flavor of this cake; the difference is that this lemon is scrumptious to eat.*

Preheat oven to 350 degrees F.

1 box Betty Crocker's Super Moist Lemon Cake mix
1 3-ounce box Jello Lemon Pudding mix
4 eggs
¾ cup canola oil
¾ cup water
⅓ cup flour
⅓ cup lemon juice

¼ cup lemon juice
2 cups powdered sugar

1. Mix together the cake mix, pudding, eggs, oil, water, flour and ¼ cup juice. Mix thoroughly for 2-3 minutes.

2. Grease a 9x13-inch pan.

3. Pour the batter evenly into the prepared pan.

4. Bake 25-30 minutes; the center of the cake will fall slightly.

5. While cake is baking, mix together the ¾ cup lemon juice and the 2 cups powdered sugar.

6. Immediately after removing the cake from the oven, poke holes with a fork all over the top of the hot cake.

7. Pour sugar/juice all over the top of the cake.

8. After 10 minutes, cover with cellophane and allow to cool prior to cutting.

# Great Grandmother's Blueberry Crumb Cake

*What can I say for a cake that has been enjoyed for more than 100 years? It is loaded with blueberries, low in fat, low in cholesterol, and there is rarely ever a piece left.*

Preheat oven to 375 degrees F.

CRUMB TOPPING:
¾ cup flour
1 cup sugar or ¾ cup sugar substitute
⅓ cup (¾ stick or 6 tablespoons) margarine
1 teaspoon cinnamon
Mix topping until tiny crumbs form and then set topping aside.

CAKE:
½ cup (1 stick) margarine
1½ cups sugar or 1⅓ cups of sugar substitute
4¼ cups plus 2 tablespoons flour
5 teaspoons baking powder
2 cups plus 2 tablespoons milk
3 cups frozen and thawed blueberries with ⅓ of the juice from the bag of frozen blueberries or 3¼ cups fresh blueberries

1. Mix together the ½ cup margarine, sugar, flour, baking powder and milk.

2. Gently add the blueberries.

3. Slowly mix all the ingredients until all the blueberries are fully incorporated.

4. Grease a 9x13-inch rectangular pan or 10x2-inch round pan

5. Pour the batter into the prepared pan.

*continued on next page*

6. Sprinkle crumb topping on top of the batter.

7. Bake approximately 50 to 65 minutes or until an inserted knife comes out clean. Allow to cool 15 minutes prior to serving.

**Variation:**
Raspberries or blackberries can be substitutes for blueberries.

# Easy Cinnamon Crumb Coffeecake

---

*One cold day, I was craving a cinnamon cake without all the fuss. I looked in my cabinet, and this recipe is what I came up with. Many a friend has enjoyed this cake, and until now they never knew that it originated from a cake mix.*

Preheat oven to 350 degrees F.

STREUSEL:
1 ¼ cups brown sugar
2 tablespoons cinnamon
¼ cup butter, melted
Mix streusel ingredients together and set aside in a separate bowl.

TOPPING:
½ cup (1 stick) butter
1 ¼ cups brown sugar
¾ plus cup flour
1 tablespoon cinnamon
Mix topping ingredients together and set aside in a separate bowl.

CAKE:
3 eggs
1 box Betty Crocker's Super Moist French Vanilla Cake mix
2 teaspoons vanilla
⅓ cup canola oil or safflower oil
1 ½ cups water
⅓ cup flour

1. Mix together all the ingredients for the cake.

*continued on next page*

2. Grease a 9x13-inch pan.

3. Spread half the batter evenly around the prepared pan.

4. Dollop the streusel by teaspoonsful all over the batter.

5. Repeat with the remaining cake batter and streusel.

6. With a butter knife, swirl the streusel around in the batter. **Do not mix! Swirl!**

7. Sprinkle topping all over the cake.

8. Bake 40-50 minutes or until an inserted knife comes out clean. Allow to cool at least 10 minutes prior to serving.

# Pecan Coffeecake

*Because I felt that I needed a nutty coffeecake, I came up with this recipe, using a combination of several different recipes. I wanted a bundt cake with lots of nuts, and this cake turned out quite good. I have yet to meet a nut fan who will turn away a piece—and who will not comment on how good it is. After experimenting with the recipe, I discovered that I had come up with a versatile cake. For a maple-flavored cake, use maple extract instead of vanilla, or for a different flavor, add diced apples to this recipe.*

Preheat oven to 350 degrees F.

FILLING:
¾ cup pecans
¾ cup brown sugar
2 tablespoons cinnamon
1 ¼ cups diced apples (optional)
Mix together the nuts, sugar, cinnamon and apples (if using apples) and set aside in a separate bowl.

CAKE:
¾ cup (1½ sticks) butter
¾ cup sugar
3 eggs
1 tablespoon vanilla or 2 teaspoons of maple extract
3 cups plus 2 tablespoons flour
1 ½ teaspoons baking powder
1 ½ teaspoons baking soda
1 ½ cups sour cream

1. Cream together the butter, sugar and eggs.

2. Add the remaining ingredients to the butter mixture and mix thoroughly.

3. Grease and flour the bottom and sides of a bundt pan.

*continued on next page*

4. Spread half the batter in the bottom of the prepared pan.

5. Sprinkle the filling all over the bottom layer of batter.

6. Top with remaining the batter. Add a pinch of cinnamon sugar on top if you wish.

7. Bake 30-40 minutes or until an inserted knife comes out clean. Allow to cool prior to serving for best flavor.

# Grandmom's Rich Coffeecake

*Personally, I prefer this recipe over my Great Grandmother's Streusel Cake, but if you find her in Heaven,
please do not tell her. Although my Great Grandmother's Streusel Cake sold better, this one has a great flavor.
If you like peaches or apples in your coffeecakes, then this recipe is the coffeecake I think you should
add them to. But adding peaches or apples is your own personal choice—this recipe tastes great
no matter what you do or do not add to it.*

Preheat oven to 325 degrees F.

CRUMB TOPPING:
½ cup (1 stick) butter
1 cup flour
1 cup plus 2 tablespoons brown sugar
2 tablespoons cinnamon
¼ teaspoon nutmeg (optional)
Mix these ingredients together and set aside in a separate bowl.

CAKE:
1 cup (2 sticks) butter
2 cups sugar
1 tablespoon vanilla
4 eggs
4¼ cups flour
4 teaspoons baking powder
1 cup sour cream
1½ cups sliced peaches or apples, drained and set aside (optional)

1. Cream together the butter, sugar, vanilla and eggs.

2. Add the flour and baking powder alternately with the sour cream to the butter mixture. Mix the
   batter thoroughly.

*continued on next page*

3. Grease a 9x13-inch pan.

4. Spread the cake batter into the prepared pan. If using fruit, place the sliced fruit on top of the batter.

5. Sprinkle the topping over the batter and fruit.

6. Bake 1 hour or until inserted an knife comes out clean. Allow to cool prior to serving.

# Great Grandmother's Carrot Cake

*If you enjoy a good and healthy carrot cake, this recipe is for you. The cream cheese icing adds an extra zip to this recipe, but is not necessary. My father shared with me that this cake was one of his favorites while he was growing up. I hope that it becomes one of your favorites, too.*

Preheat oven to 350 degrees F.

2 cups plus 2 tablespoons flour
1 cup sugar
3 eggs
¾ cup canola oil or sunflower oil
¾ cup buttermilk
20 ounce can crushed pineapple (reserve 2 tablespoons juice for the icing in a separate small bowl)
3 cups grated carrots
Additions if desired: 1 cup raisins (dark and/or golden) and/or chopped walnuts

1. Thoroughly mix all the ingredients together, except for the extra 2 tablespoons pineapple juice.

2. Grease a 9x13-inch pan

3. Pour the batter into the prepared pan.

4. Bake 40-50 minutes or until an inserted knife comes out clean. Allow to cool completely.

5. Spread the Cream Cheese Icing on the cake.

CREAM CHEESE ICING:
8 ounces cream cheese
½ cup (1 stick) butter
1 pound box powdered sugar, about 3½ cups
2 tablespoons reserved pineapple juice

*continued on next page*

1. Mix all the ingredients together.

2. Spread onto the cooled cake.

3. Refrigerate for at least 1 hour.

4. Serve and enjoy.

**Variation:**
Maple Icing also goes well with this cake; to make it, omit the pineapple juice and add 2 teaspoons maple extract to the Cream Cheese Icing.

# Peachy Streusel Coffeecake

*This is my favorite cake recipe that is made with fruit. One day, I had far too many fresh peaches that were about to go bad. These peaches desperately needed to be skinned and used, so I made up this cake recipe. When this cake is fresh out of the oven, it tastes just like a hot peach cobbler. This cake happens to be so moist that even a severe drought won't affect the moisture level!*

Preheat oven to 350 degrees F.

STREUSEL:
1 cup brown sugar
¼ cup flour
¼ cup (½ stick) butter
2 tablespoons cinnamon
¼ teaspoon nutmeg
Mix and set aside in a separate bowl.

8 cups (8-10 peaches) sliced and skinned fresh peaches or use 4 cans light peaches, drained  (To skin fresh peaches, soak them in hot water for 10-15 minutes and immediately peel the skin off.)
½ cup (1 stick) butter or margarine
1 cup sugar
2 eggs
1 tablespoon vanilla
3 cups plus 2 tablespoons flour
4 teaspoons baking powder
1 cup plus 2 tablespoons milk

1. Cream together the butter, sugar, eggs and vanilla.

2. Add flour and baking powder to the butter mixture, alternately with the milk. Mix the batter thoroughly.

3. Grease a 9x13-inch pan.

*continued on next page*

4. Spread a little less than half the batter onto the bottom of the prepared pan. You will use every bit of the batter, so when spreading batter into the pan and again on top of peaches, have a bowl of about 1 cup of flour available and a rubber spatula. Constantly repeat dipping the back of the spatula into the flour to help to spread the batter. (It will seem like there is not enough batter, but there really is enough.)

5. Sprinkle half the streusel all over the batter, and then cover the streusel with half the peaches, completely covering the bottom half of the batter.

6. Gently spread the second half of the batter over the peaches.

7. Place the remaining peaches on top of the batter, and sprinkle the remaining streusel over the peaches.

8. Bake 40-50 minutes or until an inserted knife comes out clean.

If you are like me and can't wait to taste, immediately stick a fork into the hot cake. Mmm, so good!
Be careful not to burn your tongue!

**Variation:**
Plums fresh or canned can be substituted for the peaches.

# Fresh Peach Cake

*If you prefer less sugar, and you don't have a lot of time, this is a marvelous peach cake. Although the flavor does not resemble a peach cobbler, there is still a fabulous aroma and plenty of peaches to please all. The compliments will be overflowing.*

Preheat oven to 350 degrees F.

¼ cup sugar
2 teaspoons cinnamon
Mix together and set aside in a separate bowl.

½ cup (1 stick) butter
1 ½ cups brown sugar, firmly packed
1 egg
1 teaspoon vanilla
2 cups plus 2 tablespoons flour
1 teaspoon baking soda
1 cup buttermilk
4-5 peaches skinned and diced, if the peaches are large use 4 instead of 5; or use 2 cans light, sliced peaches.
   (Drain the canned peaches, rinse twice with water and then pat dry prior to dicing.)

1. Cream together the butter, sugar, egg and vanilla.

2. Add the flour and baking soda to the butter mixture, alternately with the buttermilk. Mix the batter thoroughly.

3. Gently fold diced peaches into batter with a wooden spoon or rubber spatula.

4. Grease a 9x13-inch pan.

*continued on next page*

5. Pour the batter into the prepared pan.

6. Sprinkle cinnamon/sugar on top of batter.

7. Bake 30-35 minutes or until an inserted knife comes out clean. Allow to cool for 20 minutes prior to serving.

# Moist Apple Cake

♥

*A moist and simply easy apple cake, rich in flavor with a touch of spice.*
*This recipe is perfect to serve for a weekend brunch.*

Preheat oven to 350 degrees F.

4 cups peeled, diced apples
1½ cups sugar
2 tablespoons lemon juice
Mix together and let stand 10 minutes.

2 eggs or equivalent amount of liquid egg substitute
⅔ cups canola oil
½ teaspoon lemon peel
3 cups plus 3 tablespoons flour
2 teaspoons baking powder
2 teaspoons baking soda
1 tablespoon cinnamon
1 teaspoon nutmeg (optional)
½ teaspoon cloves
½ cup walnuts and/or raisins

1. Mix together the eggs, oil and lemon peel.

2. By hand, with a rubber spatula or wooden spoon, thoroughly mix together the flour, baking powder, baking soda, spices, nuts and/or raisins. Add the mix to the eggs and oil. Mix these ingredients together thoroughly.

3. Gently mix the apple mixture into the batter, including any juice they may have formed.

4. Grease a 9x13-inch pan.

5. Spread batter into the prepared pan.

6. Bake 35-45 minutes or until knife comes out clean. Allow to cool 20 minutes prior to serving.

# Honey Apple Cake

*This is a marvelous recipe to serve with a buffet brunch or at an after-dinner party. It is decorative, though old-fashioned, in appearance, and it tastes just as good as it looks. You may want to make more than one cake if you're serving more than six people. Serve with vanilla ice cream while the cake is hot for an extra special treat.*

Preheat oven to 375 degrees F.

3 apples peeled and sliced into ⅛-¼ inch slices
Set apple slices aside in a separate bowl.

¼ cup honey, set aside.

1 cup plus 1 tablespoon flour
1 ½ teaspoons baking powder
Pinch of salt
2 tablespoons butter
2 tablespoons honey
2 beaten egg yolks
½ cup milk
½ teaspoon nutmeg and/or cinnamon
1 teaspoon orange peel or orange zest

1. Mix together the flour, baking powder, salt, butter, 2 tablespoons honey, egg yolks and milk. Thoroughly mix the ingredients.

2. Grease a 9-inch or 10-inch round pan with a removable bottom.

3. Spread the dough all over the bottom and sides of the prepared pan.

4. Place apples in the dough with the cut side down.

5. Pour ¼ cup honey over the apples. Sprinkle ½ teaspoon nutmeg and/or cinnamon over the honey. Sprinkle 1 teaspoon of orange peel or zest over the spices.

6. Bake 30-40 minutes. Serve warm for best flavor.

# Carl's Apple Cake

*I tasted this recipe at an old friend's home a long time ago, and immediately asked him for the recipe. The combination of apples and spices was outstanding, so I adjusted the recipe for high-altitude baking requirements, and it tastes just the same as when I first sampled it. I'm sure that you will find it just as delicious as I do.*

Preheat oven to 350 degrees F.

5 large Macintosh or Fugi apples, peeled and cut into ½-inch slices
2 tablespoons cinnamon
2 tablespoons sugar
½ teaspoon nutmeg
Mix all these ingredients together and set aside in a separate bowl.

TOPPING:
½ cup brown sugar
¼ cup walnuts, pecans and/or dark raisins
2 tablespoons soft butter
1 teaspoon cinnamon
½ teaspoon nutmeg
Mix topping ingredients together and set aside in a separate bowl.

CAKE:
3 cups plus 2½ tablespoons flour
1¾ cups plus 3 tablespoons sugar
1 tablespoon baking powder
1 cup (2 sticks) butter, melted and cooled
4 beaten eggs
1 tablespoon vanilla
¼ cup orange juice

*continued on next page*

1. Thoroughly mix flour, sugar, baking powder, butter, eggs, vanilla and juice.

2. Grease a 9x13-inch pan.

3. Spread one-third of the batter into the prepared pan.

4. Cover the batter with half the apples.

5. Then spread another third of the batter over the apples, cover this layer of batter with the remaining apples, and then spread the last third of batter over the apples.

6. Sprinkle topping all over the top of the final layer of batter.

7. Bake 40-45 minutes or until an inserted knife comes out clean. Allow to cool 20 minutes prior to serving.

# Kathleen's Banana Nut/Raisin Cake

*I first enjoyed this cake while I visiting my ex in Ohio several years ago.
His Mother had baked this recipe for me. She apparently wanted to impress me with her family's
banana cake, since she knew that I baked for a living. She definitely did impress me,
for I ate two pieces my first night there and, of course, requested the recipe.*

Preheat oven to 350 degrees F.

¾ cup (1½ sticks) margarine
3 eggs
⅔ cup buttermilk
3½ large mashed bananas
¾ cup chopped walnuts and/or raisins
2½ cups flour
1⅔ cups sugar
1¼ teaspoons baking powder
1¼ teaspoons baking soda

1. Thoroughly mix the margarine, eggs, buttermilk, mashed bananas and walnuts and/or raisins.

2. Sift the flour, sugar, baking powder and baking soda into the margarine mixture. Mix the batter slowly, but thoroughly.

3. Grease and flour a 9x13-inch pan or two 9-inch round pans (if baking a layer cake).

4. Pour the batter into the prepared pans.

5. Bake 30-45 minutes, depending on choice of pan, until an inserted knife comes out clean. Allow to cool completely prior to spreading with Kathleen's White Icing.

KATHLEEN'S WHITE ICING:
½ cup sugar
¼ cup light corn syrup

2 tablespoons water
2 egg whites
1 teaspoon vanilla

1. Mix the sugar, corn syrup and water in a medium saucepan.

2. Heat mixture until it boils.

3. When sugar mixture begins to boil, turn the heat off, keep the sugar mixture on the hot range burner, and begin to beat the egg whites.

4. Beat the egg whites until stiff peaks begin to form, and then slowly pour hot sugar mixture over the egg whites and continue beating.

5. Add the vanilla and continue beating the egg white mixture until the ingredients are fully incorporated and stiff peaks are formed.

6. Spread the icing onto the cool cake and dot the top of the cake with extra chopped nuts.

# Gingerbread

*Around the first snow of the winter holiday season, my customers in the city requested that I bake them some gingerbread. I couldn't tell them I didn't have a recipe, and thus couldn't make it for them, so I began to play with ingredients. Although it took several trials and days to develop a recipe, I finally came up with the recipe below. That was about 11 years ago, and I still continue to receive special requests for my Gingerbread.*

Preheat oven to 375 degrees F.

1 cup (2 sticks) butter
1 cup sugar
4 eggs
1 cup molasses
4 cups flour
2 teaspoons baking soda
3 teaspoons cinnamon
1 teaspoon cloves
2 teaspoons ginger
1 cup buttermilk
¾ cup chopped walnuts and/or raisins (optional)

1. Cream together the butter, sugar, eggs and molasses.

2. In a separate bowl, sift together flour, baking soda and spices.

3. To the egg mixture, alternately add the sifted flour/spice mixture and the buttermilk.

4. Add the chopped walnuts and/or raisins and mix the batter thoroughly.

5. Grease a 9x13-inch pan.

6. Pour the batter into the prepared pan.

7. Bake 45-55 minutes or until an inserted knife or toothpick comes out clean. Allow to cool 20 minutes prior to serving.

# Aunt Joan's Pecan Coffeecake

*I received this recipe from a longtime friend of my Mother's, whom I will always call Aunt Joan. I first tasted this recipe when "The Ladies" were playing canasta and Aunt Joan requested my Lemon Cake recipe. She offered one of her recipes in exchange, and "The Ladies" chose this coffeecake, because they liked it so much.*

Preheat oven to 350 degrees F.

1 ½ squares unsweetened chocolate
¾ cup pecan pieces
Pinch of cinnamon
Grate or scrape chocolate into a small bowl.
Add pecans and cinnamon to the grated chocolate and mix together.
Set mixture aside.

1 box moist French Vanilla Cake mix
4 eggs
1 3-ounce box Jello Vanilla Pudding mix
1 cup sour cream
½ cup canola oil
1 tablespoon vanilla
¼ cup flour

1. Thoroughly mix all the batter ingredients together.

2. Grease and flour a bundt pan.

3. Spread half the batter onto the bottom of the prepared pan.

4. Spread chocolate/pecan mixture all over the bottom layer of batter.

5. Cover the chocolate/pecan mixture with the remaining batter.

6. Bake 50-55 minutes or until an inserted knife comes out clean. Allow to cool prior to serving.

# Cream Cheese Streusel Cake

*If you do not have an appetite for sour cream-based coffeecakes, then this is the recipe for you. It has a nice rich flavor with just the right amount of cinnamon. I prefer this cake over my Great Grandmother's, but by all means do not tell her if you happen to see her when you get to Heaven. If you have a taste for nuts or raisins in your coffeecakes, then please go ahead and add them to the streusel topping.*

Preheat oven to 350 degrees F.

STREUSEL TOPPING:
⅔ cup brown sugar
½ cup flour
1½ tablespoons cinnamon (use a little less if you prefer)
½ cup (1 stick) cold margarine
1 cup chopped nuts and/or raisins (optional)
Mix until crumbs become course or smaller than large peas. Set topping aside in a separate bowl.

CAKE:
½ cup (1 stick) margarine
8 ounces cream cheese
1 cup sugar
2 eggs
1 tablespoon vanilla
⅓ cup milk
1½ cups plus 3 tablespoons flour
1 teaspoon baking powder
½ teaspoon baking soda

1. Cream together the margarine, cream cheese and sugar.

2. Add the eggs and vanilla to the butter mixture and continue mixing. Add the remaining ingredients and mix all the ingredients together thoroughly.

3. Grease a 9x13-inch pan.

4. Spread batter evenly into pan.

5. Sprinkle the streusel topping all over the batter.

6. Bake 30-40 minutes or until an inserted knife comes out clean. Allow to cool 30 minutes prior to serving.

# Cream Cheese Chocolate-Chip Streusel Cake

---

*This recipe has yet to be turned down by anyone. Although, I have made my Mother's Chocolate Chip Cake for years for friends, I wanted a chocolate chip cake from scratch. So I played around and here is the result. My playing around with different ideas and mixtures concluded with combining a cream cheese batter with chocolate chips in both the batter and in the streusel topping. Delicious!*

Preheat oven to 350 degrees F.

STREUSEL TOPPING:
¾ cup brown sugar
¾ cup flour
⅓ cup (¾ stick) margarine
¾ cup plus mini chocolate chips
½ cup chopped nuts (optional)
In a small bowl, mix all the streusel ingredients together and stir until crumbs are course or smaller than large peas. Set streusel aside.

CAKE:
¾ cup (1½ sticks) margarine
8 ounces cream cheese
1½ cups sugar
3 eggs
1 tablespoon vanilla
¾ cup plus 2 tablespoons milk
2⅔ cups flour
1½ teaspoon baking powder
¾ teaspoon baking soda
¾ cup mini chocolate chips only (Larger chips will sink to the bottom of the cake while baking.)

1. Cream together the margarine, cream cheese and sugar.

2. Add the remaining ingredients to the margarine mixture and mix together thoroughly.

3. Grease a 9x13-inch pan.

4. Pour the batter evenly into the pan.

5. Sprinkle streusel topping evenly over batter.

6. Bake 45-55 minutes or until an inserted knife comes out clean. Allow to cool 30 minutes prior to serving.

# Mom's Chocolate-Chip Cake

*The following is probably the easiest recipe to bake in this book. It only takes five minutes to assemble and about 35-45 minutes to bake. Not bad, huh? Every time Mom made this cake for a family get-together, my cousin Leah would say "Aha! Aunt Mickey made the good cake." This cake is wonderful if you are going to a potluck outing and you do not have a lot of time on your hands but need something special to bring.*

Preheat oven to 350 degrees F.

1 box moist French Vanilla Cake mix
3 eggs or equivalent amount of liquid egg substitute
⅓ cup flour
1 tablespoon vanilla
⅓ cup canola oil
1 ⅓ cup water
⅔ cup chocolate sprinkles or mini chocolate chips (mom used sprinkles)

1. Mix together all the ingredients.

2. Grease a straight or design-sided bundt pan.

3. Pour the batter evenly into the prepared pan.

4. Bake 35-45 minutes or until an inserted knife comes out clean. Allow to cool completely prior to serving for best results.

5. Sprinkle a little powdered sugar on top of the cake prior to serving, if you like.

# Mom's Hershey Syrup Marble Cake

*When I first started baking professionally, I remember calling my Mother and requesting the Marble Cake recipe made with Hershey syrup. I wasn't sure if I could make it work at 8,000 feet above sea level, but I remembered how good it was and had to try. It took a pinch of patience on my part, but after two or three tries I got the cake to rise and not sink in the middle. Actually, I only added a tad more flour and switched the type of baking pan from a 9x13-inch pan to a bundt pan. And yes, it is well worth the trial and error effort initially put into baking this cake at high altitude.*

Preheat oven to 350 degrees F.

1 cup (2 sticks) butter
1 ¾ cups sugar
4 eggs separated, setting the whites aside in a separate mixing bowl
1 tablespoon vanilla
1 cup plus 3 tablespoons flour
1 cup plus 1 tablespoon milk
1, 16-ounce can Hershey syrup
Chocolate sprinkles or powdered sugar to sprinkle on the fully baked cake

1. Cream together the butter, sugar, egg yolks and vanilla.

2. Add the flour alternately with the milk to the butter mixture. Thoroughly mix the batter.

3. Beat egg whites until soft peaks form and then fold into the well-beaten batter.

4. Put half the batter into a smaller bowl.

5. Add the Hershey syrup into the batter remaining in the mixing bowl. Thoroughly mix the syrup into this half of the batter.

6. Grease a bundt pan.

7. By thirds, spread a layer of white batter into the prepared pan, then a layer of chocolate, then white, then chocolate, then white, then chocolate. (2 layers of each is fine if you don't want the hassle.)

*continued on next page*

8. With a butter knife, lightly swirl the vanilla and chocolate batters together to create a marble effect. **Do not mix the batters together! Swirl!**

9. Bake 50-60 minutes or until an inserted knife comes out clean.

10. Sprinkle the top of the hot cake with chocolate sprinkles. Or, when the cake is cool, sprinkle it with powdered sugar, if you like.

# Cheater's Marble Cake

*This is a very simple and quick recipe that will impress all who taste it. Your friends and family will think that you slaved for hours, although this cake takes only about 15 minutes to throw together.*

You will need 2 mixing bowls.

Preheat oven to 350 degrees F.

1 ½ cups chocolate sprinkles, set aside.

In first bowl, place the following:
1 box French Vanilla Super Moist Cake mix
3 eggs
⅓ cup canola oil
1 ⅓ cups water
¼ cup flour
2 tablespoons vanilla

In the second mixing bowl, place the following:
1 box Chocolate Fudge Super Moist Cake mix
3 eggs
⅓ cup canola oil
1 ⅓ cups water
3 tablespoons flour
3 tablespoons cocoa

1. Mix the ingredients in each separate bowl thoroughly.

2. Grease a 9x13-inch pan and 1 large-size muffin pan for individual cupcakes.

3. Cover the bottom of the prepared pan with one-third of the vanilla batter.

*continued on next page*

4. Next, drizzle one-third of the chocolate batter over the vanilla batter.

5. Then, drizzle some more of the vanilla batter, then more of the chocolate batter, then the vanilla, ending with the chocolate batter on top. (There will be extra batter of each flavor to pour into the prepared muffin pan.)

6. After layering the batters, use a knife to lightly swirl the batters to create the marble effect. **Do not mix the batters together! Swirl!**

7. Pour the extra batters into the prepared muffin pan sections, in single layers (1 layer of chocolate, and 1 layer of vanilla) and with a butter knife swirl the batters into the marbled effect. **Do not mix the batters together! Swirl!**

8. Bake the batter in the 9x13-inch pan for 45-50 minutes or until an inserted knife comes out clean. Bake the batter in the muffin pan for 15-20 minutes or until an inserted knife comes out clean.

9. Sprinkle the cake and the cupcakes with chocolate sprinkles while they are still hot. Allow to cool prior to serving.

# Marilyn's Favorite Chocolate Bundt Cake

*This is a great recipe for afternoon tea or as an after-school snack. It is easy to assemble, moist and full of good chocolate flavor. My neighbor told me she enjoys this cake because it is lighter than some other chocolate cakes she has eaten. She enjoyed the recipe so much that I decided to name it after her. This recipe can be made sugar-free for those who love chocolate but are not supposed to have too much sugar.*

Preheat oven to 350 degrees F.

¾ cup (1 ½ sticks) butter
1 ⅔ cups sugar or 1 ½ cups sugar substitute
2 eggs
1 tablespoon vanilla
1 cup sour cream or 1 cup plus 1 tablespoon plain yogurt
2 cups plus 2 tablespoons flour
¾ cup cocoa
2 teaspoons baking soda
1 cup plus 1 tablespoon buttermilk
1 cup mini chocolate chips (Larger chips will sink to the bottom of the cake.) Chopped peanut butter chips can also be used.
2 tablespoons powdered sugar, set aside (optional)

1. Cream together the butter, sugar, eggs and vanilla.

2. Add the sour cream to the butter mixture and mix.

3. To the butter mixture, add the flour, cocoa and baking soda alternately with the buttermilk.

4. Add the mini chocolate chips to the batter as the last ingredient, and thoroughly mix all the ingredients together.

5. Grease and lightly flour a bundt pan.

6. Pour the batter into the prepared pan.

*continued on next page*

7. Bake 45-50 minutes or until an inserted knife comes out clean. When the cake is cool, sprinkle the 2 tablespoons (or less) of powdered sugar on the top, if desired.

Use a paper lace doily placed on top of cooled cake for a pretty effect when sprinkling the powdered sugar.

# Kathleen's Chocolate Mayo Cake

---

*A woman, who was very dear to me, requested that her son give a family recipe notebook to me when she passed away. She knew that many of its recipes would be to my liking, especially this cake recipe. To date, it is one of the finest cakes I have ever eaten. If you like chocolate cakes, this recipe is outstanding. It works very well as a sheet cake, and it is perfect for a 9-inch layer cake.*

Preheat oven to 350 degrees F.

2 cups plus 1 tablespoon flour
⅔ cup cocoa
1 ¼ teaspoons baking soda
¼ teaspoon baking powder
Combine these ingredients in a medium bowl and set aside.

3 eggs
1 ⅔ cups sugar
1 tablespoon vanilla
1 cup plus 1 tablespoon mayonnaise
1 ⅓ cup water

1. Beat the eggs, sugar, vanilla and mayonnaise for 3-4 minutes on medium speed.

2. Add the flour mixture to the egg mixture alternately with the water. Thoroughly mix all the ingredients together.

3. Grease two 9-inch cake pans or a 9x13-inch sheet pan. Shake a tiny bit of extra flour around the pan(s) to coat the bottom and sides.

4. Pour the batter into the prepared pan(s).

5. Bake 25-40 minutes, depending on the pan size. Definitely use a toothpick or knife inserted in the middle to see if the cake is done. 1 or 2 crumbs should stick to the knife or toothpick.

*continued on next page*

6. When completely cool, apply one of the icings from the end of this chapter (starting on page 109).

Personally, I prefer the Cream Cheese Icing on this cake, whereas a friend prefers the Chocolate Icing. The choice of which icing to use is yours.

# Bob's Flourless Chocolate Cake

---

*A good friend gave me this recipe in case I had requests for flourless cake. Although I never received such a request, I tried this recipe and adjusted it to high-altitude baking. I was shocked that a cake without flour could taste so amazing. For those of you who count carbohydrates, you can still enjoy the good stuff and not feel guilty.*

Preheat oven to 350 degrees F.

12 ounces bittersweet chocolate
½ cup (1 stick) butter
2½ tablespoons dark rum
1 tablespoon vanilla
8 large, separated eggs
⅔ cup sugar
⅓ cup sugar

1. Combine the chocolate, butter, rum and vanilla in a saucepan and stir over medium heat until the chocolate and butter are completely melted.

2. Pour the chocolate mixture into a large mixing bowl.

3. In a different bowl, beat egg yolks with the ⅔ cup of sugar.

4. In a third bowl, beat egg whites with the ⅓ cup sugar until soft peaks form.

5. Fold the egg whites into the egg yolks. Mix egg mixtures together thoroughly.

6. Then, in small portions, gently fold the egg mixture into the chocolate mixture. Mix the batter thoroughly.

7. Layer a 9-inch round pan with waxed paper. Butter and lightly flour the waxed paper, and tap out any extra flour.

8. Pour the batter into the prepared pan.

9. Put the cake pan into a larger pan. Fill the larger pan halfway up the sides with warm to hot water.

*continued on next page*

10. Bake about 55-60 minutes or until an inserted knife comes out with a tiny amount of moist crumbs attached.

11. Remove cake from the pan 15 minutes after removing it from the oven. Cool completely.

12. Cover with whipped cream topping.

WHIPPED CREAM TOPPING:
2 cups whipping cream
⅓ cup powdered sugar
1 teaspoon vanilla

1. Mix these 3 ingredients together and beat until peaks form.

2. Spread Whipped Cream topping onto the cooled cake and sprinkle with chocolate sprinkles for a decorative effect.

3. Refrigerate the cake until ready to serve.

# Aunt Lil's Mother's Killer Chocolate Cake

*I will always refer to this recipe as "the best." There is nothing else to say about it. My understanding is that this recipe was my Aunt Lil's Mother's recipe. I thank either Aunt greatly, for this is a recipe to die for. When my Mother would make it, it seldom lasted more than one day. Aunt Lil's Aunt came up with an icing to go with this cake that is absolutely incredible. It is always best to make a double or even triple batch of the icing—one to eat off the spoon, one to dip fruit into and the other for the cake. (See page 97 for the icing recipe.)*

3 cups water
4 squares unsweetened chocolate
½ cup (1 stick) butter
2 cups sugar
2 cups plus 2 tablespoons flour
3 eggs
1 teaspoon vanilla
2 teaspoons baking powder

1. Bring the water to a full boil.

2. Measure out 1¼ cups, discard the remaining water and add the 4 squares of unsweetened chocolate to the 1¼ cups of hot water. Mix the chocolate and water together until all the chocolate is melted and let the mixture cool.

3. Cream together the butter, sugar and flour.

4. Mix the chocolate/water into the butter mixture and blend thoroughly.

5. Then, refrigerate the chocolate and butter mixture for 1 hour.

6. Preheat oven to 325 degrees F.

7. Remove the chocolate/butter mixture from the refrigerator, and add the eggs, 1 egg at a time, until all the eggs are fully incorporated into the batter. Add the vanilla to the batter and mix.

8. Mix the baking powder into the batter with a rubber spatula, wooden spoon or fork. Mix all the ingredients together thoroughly.

*continued on next page*

9. Grease a 9x13-inch pan.

10. Pour the batter evenly into the prepared pan.

11. Bake the cake 50-60 minutes or until an inserted knife comes out clean. Let cake cool prior to pouring and spreading Aunt Lil's Aunt's Chocolate Icing (page 97) onto the cake.

Powdered sugar can be sprinkled over cooled cake instead of using the icing.

# Aunt Lil's Aunt's Chocolate Icing for the Killer Chocolate Cake

*As a little girl, knowing that I would get my hand slapped, I would always stick my fingers or a spoon into this icing while it was still hot. I thought it was some of the best stuff on earth, and still do. As an adult, I have found that if kept warm, this recipe makes the most incredible chocolate fondue I have ever tasted. For the ultimate match, use this icing for the Killer Chocolate Cake on page 95.*

2 squares unsweetened chocolate

2 tablespoons butter

½ cup sugar

1, 5-ounce can evaporated milk (If doubling recipe or more, go to 10 ounces, 15 ounces and so on)

2 teaspoons vanilla

1. In a double boiler, melt the chocolate and butter.

2. After the chocolate and butter are melted, add the sugar, evaporated milk and vanilla. Stir constantly over medium heat until mixture thickens, approximately 30 minutes.

3. Remove the icing from the heat and while still warm, pour and spread the icing all over the cooled cake. Allow the icing to cool prior to serving.

# Chocolate Fondue Cake

*For those of you who prefer a more decadent chocolate cake simply add fruit to the top of Aunt Lil's Mother's Killer Chocolate Cake prior to adding Aunt Lil's Aunt's Chocolate Icing. This absolutely wonderful cake is sure to make an everlasting impression on all who try it.*

1. Follow the recipe for Aunt Lil's Mother's Killer Chocolate cake on page 95.

2. Put 2 cups of desired fruit on top of the cooled cake prior to pouring and spreading Aunt Lil's Aunt's Chocolate Icing. Raspberries, strawberries, cherries, bananas, blackberries or blueberries work best.

If using bananas, sprinkle a few drops of lemon juice over the sliced bananas; mix the bananas and lemon juice together prior to placing them on the cake. (The bananas will keep better this way.)

# Chocolate Cream Cheese Cake

*This recipe is a classic example of two astounding flavors uniting into one yummy cake. Looking and tasting beautiful, this cake will absolutely impress any guests invited to your table.*

Preheat oven to 350 degrees F.

12 ounces cream cheese
⅓ cup sugar
1 teaspoon vanilla
1 egg

½ cup (1 stick) butter
1½ cups sugar
3 eggs
2 cups flour
⅔ cup cocoa
1 cup water
1 tablespoon vanilla
1¼ teaspoons baking powder
1 teaspoon baking soda

1. Cream together the cream cheese, sugar, vanilla and 1 egg in a separate bowl. Set the cream cheese mixture aside.

2. Thoroughly mix the remaining ingredients together in another bowl.

3. Grease and lightly flour a large bundt pan.

4. Pour half the chocolate cake batter into the prepared pan.

5. Spread all the cream cheese mixture over the bottom chocolate layer. (Try not to touch the sides of pan with any cream cheese mixture.)

*continued on next page*

6. Pour the remaining chocolate batter over the cream cheese mixture.

7. Bake 50-60 minutes or until an inserted knife comes out clean. Allow the cake to cool and remove from the pan. Drizzle topping over cake after it cools and is removed from pan.

TOPPING:
¼ cup chocolate chips
2 teaspoons butter
2½ teaspoons milk
2 pieces of a Hershey's milk chocolate bar

3 ounces white chocolate
1 teaspoon melted butter

1. Melt together the first 4 ingredients.

2. Mix well and drizzle over the cooled cake.

3. Then, melt together the white chocolate and butter and mix together.

4. Drizzle the white chocolate mixture over the cake.

5. Let chocolates dry completely prior to serving.

# Dump It Cake

*I first heard of this cake after a dear friend sent me her family cooking notebook. Not only did it sound silly to me, it sounded awfully sweet. Actually, it is rather tasty and fruity. This is a fun cake to make with children. They get a kick out of the name and are pleasantly surprised when tasting the results of all the "dumping."*

Preheat oven to 350 degrees F.

1 large can cherry pie filling
1 20-ounce can crushed pineapple
1 box super Moist Yellow Cake mix
½ cup (1 stick) margarine
8 ounces coconut (optional)

1. Grease a 9x13-inch cake pan.

2. Dump the cherry pie filling into the pan and spread it around.

3. Dump the crushed pineapple on top of the cherries and spread it around. If using coconut, sprinkle it over the fruit.

4. Next, sprinkle the cake mix evenly over the other ingredients, covering the pan entirely.

5. Thinly slice the stick of margarine over the entire pan.

6. Bake about 40 minutes. The cake will be done when it's nice and brown on top. Allow to cool prior to serving.

# Plain Ole Yellow Layer Cake

*This is a worthy, all-purpose cake that can be eaten as is, or you can add fruits, jams or nuts to the middle layer and add your choice of icing. I use Cream Cheese Icing with freshly sliced strawberries or cherries in the center. Yum!*

Preheat oven to 350 degrees F.

¾ cup (1½ sticks) butter or margarine
1 cup sugar
1 tablespoon vanilla
8 egg yolks
2½ cups flour
1 tablespoon baking powder
¾ cup of milk

1. Cream together the butter, sugar, vanilla and egg yolks.

2. Add the flour and baking powder alternately with the milk. Thoroughly mix the batter.

3. Grease two or three 9-inch pans, depending on the number of layers desired. (Remember, the more layers you have, the thinner each layer will be.)

4. Bake 20-30 minutes or until a knife inserted in the center comes out clean.

5. Cool and frost as desired. Icing recipes start on page 109.

# Hazelnut Cake

*This is a perfect cake to bake during the Christmas season. Rich in hazelnuts (filberts) and topped with a delightful icing developed for this cake. Decorate the top of this cake with candied red and green cherries and holly leaves for a festive finishing touch.*

Preheat oven to 325 degrees F.

2 cups sugar
⅔ cup (1⅓ sticks) butter
4 eggs
1 tablespoon vanilla
2⅔ cups flour
2 teaspoons baking powder
1 cup milk
1 cup chopped hazelnuts (To chop the nuts, either place them in a food processor and chop, or do as I do, and put the nuts in a freezer Ziploc bag and repetitively beat them with a rolling pin or a rubber hammer until you reach a desired size. Do not grate the nuts, only chop.)

1. Beat the sugar, butter, eggs and vanilla on medium speed for 2-3 minutes.

2. Add the flour and baking powder alternately with the milk to the butter mixture.

3. Mix batter and stir in the chopped hazelnuts. Thoroughly mix all the ingredients.

4. Grease and flour two 9-inch round pans or a 9x13-inch cake pan.

5. Pour the batter evenly into the pan(s).

6. Bake 45-55 minutes or until an inserted knife comes out clean.

7. Cool and frost.

*continued on next page*

HAZELNUT CAKE FROSTING:
½ cup soft butter
1 cup brown sugar, well-packed
⅓ cup heavy cream
2 cups powdered sugar
1 tablespoon vanilla

1. Beat all the ingredients together until they reach a smooth and spreadable consistency.

2. Spread icing on the cooled cake.

3. Decorate the top of the frosting with candied cherries and holly leaves for a pretty effect (optional).

# Aunt Lil's Cheesecake

*In Aunt Lil's words "It's a super good cake; everyone enjoys it." She also says, "This cake is perfect for entertaining a lot of people."*

Preheat oven to 350 degrees F.

THE CRUST:
½ cup (1 stick) butter
1 ¾ cups graham cracker crumbs

1. Melt butter and mix with the graham cracker crumbs.

2. Grease a springform pan well.

3. Pat graham cracker mixture onto the bottom and partially up the sides of the prepared pan.

4. Set the pan aside.

FILLING:
(Please, follow the directions exactly as they are written.)

1. Beat well in a mixing bowl
   16 ounces cream cheese and 1 pint sour cream (2 cups)

2. Then, in a separate mixing bowl, mix together:
   1 cup sugar
   1 tablespoon flour

3. Then, separate 5 eggs into 2 bowls, the yolks in one and the whites in a separate bowl.

4. Mix the egg yolks in with the sugar/flour mixture.

5. Add the following two ingredients to the egg yolk mixture:
   2 teaspoons lemon juice
   1 teaspoon vanilla
   And mix thoroughly.

*continued on next page*

6. Then, mix the egg yolks and sugar mixture thoroughly into the cream cheese/sour cream mixture.

7. Beat the egg whites until soft peaks form.

8. Completely fold egg whites into the cream cheese mixture. **Do not beat—fold!**

9. Pour the cream cheese batter on top of the graham cracker crust.

10. Bake for about 1 hour, then turn the oven off, open the door and let the cake sit in the warm oven for another hour. The cake will sink slightly in the middle.

11. Allow the cake to cool; refrigerate the cake for 24 hours before serving.

# Cheesecake

---

*I love a good cheesecake, but I did not have a recipe when I came up with this one. (At the time I developed this recipe, I did not have my Aunt Lil's Cheesecake recipe.) I began playing around with a variety of the necessary ingredients. The following is the result of my cheerful but fattening adventures while developing a really good and easy-to-bake cheesecake.*

Preheat oven to 350 degrees F.

THE CRUST:
1 cup ground graham crackers  (The cinnamon version works great.)
3 tablespoons sugar
3 tablespoons melted butter

1. Mix the crackers, sugar and butter together.

2. Completely butter the sides and bottom of a 9-inch springform pan.

3. Tightly wrap foil over the entire bottom and partially up the outer sides of the pan.

4. Press the graham crumb mixture all over the bottom and partially up the inner sides of the pan. Set the prepared pan aside.

FILLING:
4, 8-ounce packages cream cheese
1½ cups sugar
4 eggs
¼ cup flour
½ tablespoon vanilla
2 drops lemon juice
¾ cup whipping cream

*continued on next page*

1. Cream the cream cheese, sugar and eggs (adding 1 egg at a time) for 2-3 minutes.

2. Add the flour, vanilla, lemon juice and whipping cream to the cream cheese mixture and continue mixing for another 3-4 minutes.

3. Pour the cream cheese batter on top of the prepared crust.

4. Fill a pan larger than the cheesecake pan with a small amount of water about ½-inch deep.

5. Place the cheesecake pan into the pan with water, making sure the water level does not go more than halfway up the sides of the cheesecake pan.

6. Place the pans in the oven and bake about 1 hour or until the cake barely jiggles when lightly shaken.

7. Remove from the oven and allow the cake to cool for about 45 minutes.

8. Cover the cake with cellophane and refrigerate for about 24 hours prior to serving.

# Cake Icings

*I have learned, through much experimentation, that the following icing recipes work beautifully with several of the cake recipes in this book. Choose whichever one suits your fancy—they are all wonderfully easy to prepare and exceptionally good.*

## 1.

CHOCOLATE ICING:

6 squares unsweetened chocolate
½ cup (1 stick) butter
4 cups powdered sugar
2 teaspoons vanilla
½ cup heavy cream

1. Melt the chocolate and butter together, over hot water on the stove or in the microwave.

2. Add the sugar and vanilla to the melted chocolate and beat together until thick and creamy.

3. Add the heavy cream and continue beating the ingredients until icing reaches a smooth and creamy spreading consistency.

**Variation to the Chocolate Icing:**
Add 8 ounces of cream cheese to the chocolate mixture and blend into the icing.

## 2.

CREAM CHEESE ICING:

Use for layer cakes or the Carrot Cake.
16 ounces cream cheese
1 cup (2 sticks) butter
4 cups powdered sugar
1 tablespoon vanilla
½ cup heavy cream

*continued on next page*

1. Beat cream cheese, butter, sugar and vanilla until thick and creamy.

2. Add the heavy cream and continue beating until the mixture reaches a smooth and creamy spreading consistency.

## 3.

LEMON ICING:
Follow the recipe for Cream Cheese Icing starting on page 109, and add:
½ cup additional powdered sugar
⅓ cup fresh lemon juice
1 teaspoon grated lemon peel or fresh lemon zest
1 teaspoon lemon extract

1. Mix all the ingredients thoroughly until icing reaches a smooth and creamy spreading consistency.

## 4.

WHITE ICING:
Double this recipe when using for a layer cake.
2⅔ cups powdered sugar
⅓ cup (¾ stick or 6 tablespoons) butter
1 tablespoon vanilla
⅓ cup milk or, for a thicker icing, use ⅓ cup heavy cream

1. Beat all ingredients thoroughly for 3 minutes on medium. If icing appears too thick, add 1 tablespoon of heavy cream at a time until icing reaches the desired spreading consistency.

## 5.

MAPLE ICING:
Double this recipe if using for a layer cake.
2 cups powdered sugar
2 tablespoons butter

1 teaspoon vanilla

1½ teaspoons maple extract

½ cup pure maple syrup, not imitation

1. Beat all the ingredients together until the icing reaches a smooth and creamy spreading consistency

# 6.

WHIPPED CREAM ICING:

3 cups heavy cream

2-3 cups powdered sugar (the amount depends on how sweet you like your icing)

1 tablespoon vanilla

1. Beat heavy cream 3-4 minutes or until stiff peaks form.

2. Add sugar and vanilla and continue beating until icing reaches a thick and creamy spreading consistency.

This icing must remain cool. Immediately after spreading this icing onto the cake, refrigerate the cake until it is served.

# 7.

CARAMEL ICING:

Double this recipe when using for a layer cake.

1 cup brown sugar

½ cup sugar

3 tablespoons milk or half-and-half

2 teaspoons vanilla

1. Put all the ingredients into a quart size saucepan and cook on medium.

2. Continue cooking while stirring constantly until ingredients begin to thicken.

3. Cook 1-2 more minutes until mixture reaches a spreadable consistency. Add 1 tablespoon powdered sugar if the icing appears too thin to spread on the cake.

4. Spread icing evenly, while warm, on the chosen cake.

# The Legend of the Mountain Muffin

High up in the Rockies 'neath the Colorado night sky,

the aroma of fresh-baked muffins wafted through curtains

of falling snow.  For miles around, folks knew that the Muffin Lady was

at it again... turning natural country fixin's

(like the finest fruits, spices and nuts, the freshest

butter and eggs) into mouth watering treats.

The recipe was a secret handed down from long ago.

Carried on the wind through the aspens to her ears alone

so they say. A pinch of this, a pinch of that for home-baked flavor

and goodness. Yours today and every day with

Mountain Muffins.

**The Muffin Lady**

**Old Fashioned Treats**

Evergreen, CO

*Call me down the shore*
*Dad*

# Mountain Muffins

* All recipes can be doubled or tripled.
* When baking at high altitude, please remember that baked goods tend to dry out quickly. After baking muffins, either serve them immediately, place them in a Ziploc bag, or wrap individually in cellophane while still a tad warm for best results. I prefer to wrap the large muffins in cellophane, for in a Ziploc bag they have a tendency to stick together.
* All the muffins on the following pages can be frozen for up to eight days.

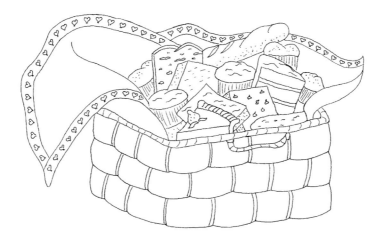

**Clockwise from top:** Blueberry, Berry Berry, Almond Chocolate Chip, Lemon Poppyseed

**Small Bowl:** Mini Almond Chocolate Chip

# Cheese and Broccoli Muffins

♥

*This recipe is wonderful for a morning snack or served as an accompaniment with soup or dinner. The muffins have a wonderful cheesy flavor and are extremely versatile. This recipe can be prepared with almost any additions your palate or meal calls for.*

Preheat oven to 375 degrees F.

½ cup (1 stick) melted margarine or canola oil (I use margarine)
2 tablespoons sugar
2 cups plus 2 tablespoons flour
3 diced scallions
2 eggs or equivalent amount of liquid egg substitute
2 teaspoons baking powder
¾ cup plus 1 tablespoon milk
¾ cup shredded Cheddar or Swiss cheese
2 ounces cream cheese, cut into pieces
¾ cup chopped broccoli, cooked and drained
½ teaspoon garlic powder
¾ teaspoon dill weed
Salt and pepper (optional)

1. At slow speed, mix all the ingredients until thoroughly combined.

2. Grease 4-5 sections of a large muffin tin.

3. Fill each muffin section ⅞ full with the batter.

4. Bake 25-35 minutes or until an inserted toothpick comes out clean but moist. Serve warm for best flavor.

Add 1 extra egg when doubling and add 2 extra eggs when tripling this recipe.

*continued on next page*

**Variations:**

* Substitute spinach, cooked and chopped, for the broccoli.

* Substitute 3 large pieces crumbled bacon or ⅔ cup diced ham for the broccoli.

* Substitute 2 drops hot sauce and 2 teaspoons chopped and diced jalapeños and ¼ cup diced green pepper for the broccoli. With this combination, use only cheddar or pepper jack cheese.

# Grandmom's Zucchini Muffins

*This recipe has always been one of the most popular of all the muffins I bake. With the combination of baking spices, they have such an awesome flavor and they smell so good that my vet thinks I should turn the recipe into perfume. Remember, when giving these muffins to little kids, have them taste the muffins first, prior to informing them that they are made from a "vegetable" or you may get a "eeuuw," and they will never know how good the muffins really are.*

Preheat oven to 350 degrees F.

1 cup canola or safflower oil
1 cup sugar
1 cup firmly packed brown sugar
2 tablespoons vanilla
3 eggs or equivalent amount of liquid egg substitute
⅓ cup molasses
2¼ cups grated zucchini
3 cups plus 2 tablespoons flour
1 teaspoon baking soda
¼ teaspoon baking powder
1 tablespoon cinnamon
1 teaspoon nutmeg
½ teaspoon cloves
¾ cup raisins, chocolate chips and/or chopped walnuts (optional)

1. Mix together the oil, sugars, vanilla, eggs, molasses and zucchini.
2. Add the flour, baking soda, baking powder, spices and choice of raisins, walnuts and/or chocolate chips to the sugar mixture. Mix all the ingredients for 2-3 minutes to make sure they are fully incorporated into the batter.

*continued on next page*

3. Grease 5-6 sections of a large muffin tin or 12 regular size muffin sections.

4. Fill each muffin section to the top with the batter.

5. Bake 30-40 minutes or until an inserted toothpick comes out clean. Let muffins cool 10 minutes prior to serving.

Add 1 extra egg when doubling and add 2 extra eggs when tripling this recipe.

# Great Grandmother's Berry Berry Muffins

*This is one of the best muffin recipes I found in my Grandmom's Tin Box. Originally, this recipe was called Strawberry Muffins. I altered the recipe a bit for high altitude, and added a mixture of different berries to discover that the Berry Berry Muffins sold the best. Nevertheless, I prefer the straight strawberry. My Father, however, preferred the straight blackberry. It is a matter of personal preference as to which berries to choose for this recipe. No matter which flavor you decide to use, this is a moist and tasty muffin—and much healthier for you than grabbing a candy bar or doughnut for a snack.*

Preheat oven to 350 degrees F.

Use only frozen or fresh-frozen fruit.

1 bag of frozen mixed berries, thawed or ⅔ cup of each: fresh frozen blueberries, raspberries, blackberries and strawberries, thawed together in a microwave (Do not drain the juice.)
4 eggs or equivalent amount of liquid egg substitute
1 cup canola oil
2 cups sugar or 1¾ cups sugar substitute
3¼ cups flour
1 teaspoon baking soda

1. Mix together the eggs, oil, sugar, and half the fruit with the juice. Thoroughly mix these ingredients for 2 minutes.
2. Add the flour and baking soda alternately with the remaining fruit and juice to the oil and egg mixture. If batter appears too liquidity, add 2 tablespoons more flour.
3. Grease 6 large muffin pan sections or 12 regular size muffin pan sections or about 2 dozen plus mini muffin pan sections.
4. Fill each section ⅞ full with the batter.
5. Bake 25-45 minutes (depending on muffin size) until firm to touch or when an inserted toothpick comes out clean.

*continued on next page*

**Variations:**

* For individual fruit-flavored muffins (for example, just blueberry) use a ¼ cup more fruit and juice combined.
* For plain strawberry muffins, add 2 teaspoons vanilla and 1½ teaspoons cinnamon.
* For plain raspberry muffins, add 2 teaspoons vanilla.

Add 1 extra egg when doubling or add 2 extra eggs when tripling this recipe.

# Jalapeño Corn Muffins

*Many years ago I got this recipe from a friend in graduate school. We were making chili one night, and I asked her if she knew how to make corn muffins. She said yes, that her mother had a great recipe. I made a few adjustments, and here lies the result. These muffins are a perfect complement to chili or black bean soup.*

Preheat oven to 375 degrees F.

3 cups corn meal
3 cups flour
⅓ cup sugar
1 tablespoon baking powder
1½ teaspoons baking soda
1½ teaspoons cayenne pepper
5 eggs
¾ cup (1½ sticks) melted butter
3 teaspoon diced jalapeños
3⅓ cups buttermilk

1. Mix together the dry ingredients in a mixing bowl.

2. Add the eggs, butter and jalapeños to the dry ingredients while gradually adding the buttermilk and mix the batter thoroughly.

3. Grease 8 large muffin sections or 12 regular size muffin sections.

4. Fill each muffin section to the top with the batter.

5. Bake 25-35 minutes or until an inserted toothpick comes out clean. Best served warm.

**Variations:**

CHEESE CORN MUFFINS:

1. Follow same directions as above.

2. Add 1 cup shredded cheddar and ½ cup corn kernels with the eggs and buttermilk. (Jalapeños optional.)

# Grandmom's Carrot Muffins

*This recipe also came out of my Grandmom's Tin Box. They are everything carrot muffins should be—healthy, moist and flavorful with just the right amount of spice.*

Preheat oven to 375 degrees F.

2 cups grated carrots
1, 8-ounce can crushed pineapple and the juice
2 eggs or equivalent amount of liquid egg substitute
½ cup canola oil
⅔ cup firmly packed brown sugar
1 tablespoon vanilla
⅓ cup raisins and/or pecans
1¾ cups flour
1 teaspoon baking powder
½ teaspoon baking soda
1 tablespoon cinnamon
½ teaspoon each nutmeg and clove

1. Thoroughly mix the carrots, pineapple, eggs, oil, sugar and vanilla.

2. Add the remaining ingredients to the carrot mixture and mix thoroughly.

3. Grease 4-5 large muffin pan sections or 9 regular size muffin pan sections.

4. Fill each muffin section ⅞ full with the batter.

5. Bake 25-35 minutes or until an inserted toothpick comes out clean.

Add 1 extra egg when doubling or add 2 extra eggs when tripling this recipe.

# Apple/Carrot Muffins

♥

*I came up with this recipe after I receiving many requests from down in the city for this combination of flavors. It wasn't very hard to come up with, and has been enjoyed ever since. This muffin is perfect for a winter holiday brunch.*

Preheat oven to 375 degrees F.

1 cup grated carrots
1 cup grated apples (preferably Granny Smith apples)
1 8-ounce can crushed pineapple and juice
2 eggs or equivalent amount of liquid egg substitute
½ cup canola oil
⅔ cup firmly packed brown sugar
1 tablespoon vanilla
¾ cup raisins and/or chopped pecans (optional)
1¾ cups flour
1 teaspoon baking powder
½ teaspoon baking soda
1 tablespoon cinnamon
½ teaspoon each nutmeg and clove

1. Thoroughly mix the carrots, apples, crushed pineapples and juice, eggs, oil, sugar and vanilla.

2. Add the remaining ingredients to the carrot/apple mixture and mix thoroughly.

3. Grease 5 sections of large muffin pan sections or 9-10 regular size muffin pan sections or 2 dozen mini muffin pan sections.

4. Fill muffin sections ⅞ full with the batter.

5. Bake 25-35 minutes or until an inserted toothpick comes out clean.

For a double batch, use only 3 eggs.

# Great Grandmother's Apple Muffins

*This is the item that I, The Muffin Lady, got started with. I found the recipe in my Grandmom's Tin Box and knew immediately from the handwriting that it was my Great Grandmother's recipe. I took these muffins as a sample of my goods to the very first place where I sold baked goods. They loved them on the spot. This recipe makes fabulous mini muffins for a weekend brunch or for a potluck picnic. Enjoy!*

Preheat oven to 350 degrees F.

½ cup sugar
½ cup canola or sunflower oil
2 eggs or equivalent amount of liquid egg substitute
1 tablespoon vanilla
1 tablespoon lemon juice
1 teaspoon lemon peel
2 cups plus 2 tablespoons grated Granny Smith apples
1⅓ cups flour
1 teaspoon baking soda
1 tablespoon cinnamon
½ teaspoon each nutmeg and cloves
¾ cup chopped pecans or raisins

1. Thoroughly mix the sugar, oil, eggs, vanilla, lemon juice and lemon peel.

2. Add the flour, baking soda, spices and raisins and/or pecans alternately with the grated apples to the sugar mixture. Thoroughly mix the batter.

3. Grease 4-5 large muffin sections or 9-10 regular size muffin pan sections or 2 dozen mini muffin pan sections.

4. Fill each muffin section to the top with the batter, and if using pecans, sprinkle some chopped nuts on top of each muffin.

5. Bake 15-35 minutes (depending on the size of muffin sections) or until an inserted toothpick comes out clean.

These muffins will not get much height to them.

Add 1 extra egg when doubling or add 2 extra eggs when tripling this recipe.

# Grandmom's Blueberry Muffins

*What would a baking recipe book be without a blueberry muffin recipe? Blueberry muffins have been a favorite of blueberry lovers for centuries. This recipe book has a few different blueberry muffin recipes; the choice of which muffin recipe you prefer is personal. This muffin is a beautiful old-fashioned recipe, plain and simple, with loads of berries.*

Preheat oven to 375 degrees F.

½ cup (1 stick) melted margarine
1½ cups sugar
4 eggs
2 cups milk
1 tablespoon vanilla
4¼ cups flour
2 tablespoons baking powder
1 teaspoon baking soda
3½ cups fresh or thawed frozen blueberries and some juice if using frozen fruit

1. Thoroughly mix the melted margarine, sugar, eggs, milk and vanilla.

2. Add the dry ingredients to the egg mixture alternately with the blueberries.

3. Grease 10-12 large muffin sections or 24 regular size muffin pan sections or 3 dozen mini muffin pan sections.

4. Fill each muffin section ⅞ full with the batter.

5. Bake 15-35 minutes (depending on the size of muffin sections), until firm to touch or an inserted toothpick comes out clean.

Add 1 extra egg when doubling or add 2 extra eggs when tripling this recipe.

# Cranberry Muffins

*Although everyone enjoyed my Grandmom's Blueberry Muffins, cranberry muffins were always requested in the fall. So I followed the Blueberry Muffins recipe but substituted cranberries for blueberries and added a pinch of orange zest. Ah, the result is delightful.*

Preheat oven to 375 degrees F.

½ cup (1 stick) melted margarine
1½ cups sugar
4 eggs
2 cups milk
1 tablespoon vanilla
4¼ cups flour
2 tablespoons baking powder
1 teaspoon baking soda
1 teaspoon orange peel or orange zest
4 cups fresh or frozen and thawed cranberries
¾ cup chopped walnuts (optional)

1. Thoroughly mix the melted margarine, sugar, eggs, milk and vanilla.

2. To the egg mixture, add the dry ingredients and orange peel alternately with the cranberries.

3. Grease 9-10 large muffin sections or 16-18 regular size muffin pan sections or 3 dozen mini muffin pan sections.

4. Fill muffin sections ⅞ full with the batter.

5. Bake 15-35 minutes (depending on the size of muffin sections), until firm to touch or until an inserted toothpick comes out clean.

Add 1 extra egg when doubling or add 2 extra eggs when tripling this recipe.

# Sweet, Dark, Red Cherry Muffins

*As I said before, cherries are my favorite fruit, so of course I had to come up with a good cherry muffin recipe. These muffins happen to be quite moist and are best enjoyed after they are completely cool. If you like cherries, these are the muffins for you.*

Preheat oven to 375 degrees F.

¼ cup (½ stick) melted margarine
¾ cups sugar
2 eggs
1 cup milk
2 teaspoons vanilla
1 teaspoon almond extract
2¼ cups flour
1 tablespoon baking powder
½ teaspoon baking soda
1¼ cups fresh and pitted or frozen and thawed dark, red cherries
⅓ cup sliced almonds

1. Thoroughly mix the melted margarine, sugar, eggs, milk, vanilla and almond extract.

2. Add the dry ingredients to the egg mixture alternately with the cherries.

3. Grease 4-5 large muffin sections or 12 regular size muffin pan sections.

4. Fill muffins sections ⅞ full with the batter. Sprinkle almond slices on top of each muffin.

5. Bake 20-35 minutes (depending on the size of muffin sections), until firm to touch or until an inserted toothpick comes out clean.

# Almond Poppyseed or Almond Chocolate-Chip Muffins

*Once again, I altered a basic recipe of my Grandmom's and the results turned out beautifully.
Whether choosing to bake Almond Poppyseed Muffins or Almond Chocolate-Chip Muffins this recipe is
fantastic. The delectable combination of almonds and chocolate has been a favorite, probably as far back as
when the cocoa bean was discovered. Hence, this treasured union is in the form of the recipe is below.
On the other hand, poppyseed muffins are also a treasured delight. The choice of which flavor to make is yours.
These muffins work beautifully as mini muffins for a brunch or any type of get-together.
This recipe tastes best when served and eaten the same day the muffins are baked.*

Preheat oven to 375 degrees F.

¼ cup (½ stick) melted margarine
¾ cups sugar
2 eggs
1 cup milk
1 teaspoon vanilla
1½ teaspoons almond extract
2¼ cups flour
1 tablespoon baking powder
½ teaspoon baking soda
¼ cup poppy seeds or ⅓ cup mini chocolate chips
⅓ cup sliced almonds

1. Thoroughly mix the melted margarine, sugar, eggs, milk, vanilla and almond extract.

2. Add the dry ingredients and poppyseeds, if using, to the egg mixture. If using chocolate chips, add them with the dry ingredients. Thoroughly mix the batter until all ingredients are fully incorporated.

*continued on next page*

3. Grease 5-6 large muffin pan sections or 10-12 regular size muffin pan sections or 2 dozen mini muffin sections.

4. Fill each muffin section ⅞ full with the batter. Sprinkle almond slices on top of each muffin.

5. Bake 15-35 minutes until firm on top or until an inserted toothpick comes out clean.

Add 1 extra egg when doubling or add 2 extra eggs when tripling this recipe.

# Lemon Poppyseed Muffins

*And again, I altered a basic recipe and it turned out wonderfully! Moist and lemony, these muffins are best eaten while still warm, or at least the same day they are baked. High altitude has a tendency to dry the recipe out quickly—but don't worry, these muffins will not last long enough to dry out. Similar to the Almond Poppyseed Muffins recipe on page 129, this one works beautifully as mini muffins.*

Preheat oven to 375 degrees F.

¼ cup (½ stick) melted margarine
¾ cups sugar
2 eggs
1 cup milk
2 ½ tablespoons lemon juice
1 teaspoon lemon extract
1 heaping tablespoon lemon curd
2 ¼ cups flour
1 tablespoon baking powder
½ teaspoon soda
¼ cup poppy seeds

1. Thoroughly mix the melted margarine, sugar, eggs, milk, lemon juice, lemon extract and lemon curd.

2. Add the dry ingredients and poppyseeds to the egg mixture. Thoroughly mix batter until all ingredients are fully incorporated.

3. Grease 5-6 large muffin pan sections or 10-12 regular size muffin pan sections or 2 dozen mini muffin sections.

4. Fill each muffin section ⅞ full with the batter.

5. Bake 15-35 minutes (depending on the size of muffin sections), until firm to touch or until an inserted toothpick comes out clean.

*continued on next page*

Add 1 extra egg when doubling or add 2 extra eggs when tripling this recipe.

**Variations:**
Omit the poppy seeds and add 1 cup fresh raspberries or blueberries sprinkled with a pinch of flour prior to adding to the batter.

# Peach Muffins

*This happens to be one of the best peach muffins I have ever tasted, and it is my favorite muffin. Light, moist and fruity, what else can you ask for in a basic everyday muffin? These do not freeze well because of all the fruit, so they are best eaten within two days of being baked. Allow to cool for a few minutes prior to tasting.*

Preheat oven to 375 degrees F.

¼ cup (½ stick) melted margarine
¾ cup sugar
2 eggs
1 cup milk
1 tablespoon vanilla
1 cup plus 2 tablespoons diced fresh or canned peaches (If using canned, **do not** use peaches in heavy syrup—use light syrup or peaches canned in water; drain any syrup/water before using.)
2¼ cups flour
1 tablespoon baking powder
½ teaspoon baking soda
¼ teaspoon nutmeg

1. Thoroughly mix the margarine, sugar, eggs, milk, vanilla and diced peaches.

2. Add the dry ingredients to the egg mixture alternately with the peaches. Thoroughly mix batter until all ingredients are fully incorporated.

3. Grease 5-6 large muffin pan sections or 10-12 regular size muffin pan sections.

4. Fill each muffin section ⅞ full with the batter.

5. Bake 25-35 minutes (depending on the size of muffin sections) until firm to touch or until an inserted toothpick comes out clean.

Add 1 extra egg when doubling or add 2 extra eggs when tripling this recipe.

# Bob Jackson's Favorite Blueberry Muffins

*Mr. Jackson is not only a dear friend, but he is the biggest fan of blueberry muffins I have ever met. He has tasted all of my various blueberry muffin recipes and gladly determined that this recipe tasted the best. As a result of his taste testing, this is the recipe I use when blueberry muffins are requested. There are a number of reasons that make this recipe fabulous: it has been used for at least 100 years, these muffins are low in fat and cholesterol, and the recipe is quite easy to assemble and bake.*

Preheat oven to 375 degrees F.

⅓ cup (¾ stick) margarine
1 cup sugar or ¾ cup plus 2 tablespoons sugar substitute
1 tablespoon vanilla
1⅓ cups plus 1 tablespoon milk
3 cups plus 2 tablespoons flour
3¾ teaspoons baking powder
1¾ cups fresh or frozen blueberries

1. Thoroughly mix together the margarine, sugar, vanilla, milk, flour and baking powder.

2. Add the blueberries last. Gently, at slow speed, mix berries thoroughly into the batter.

3. Grease 8 sections of a large muffin pan or 12 regular size muffin sections.

4. Fill each muffin section to top with batter.

TOPPING:
Combine:
  2 tablespoons sugar or sugar substitute
  2 tablespoons flour
  1 teaspoon cinnamon

5. Sprinkle the cinnamon mixture on top of each muffin.

6. Bake 20-35 minutes (depending on the size of muffin sections), until they are golden and feel firm on top or until an inserted knife or toothpick comes out clean.

**Variation:**
Raspberries or diced peaches can be used in place of berries.

# Chocolate Chocolate-Chip Muffins

*For a chocolate muffin, this recipe makes the top of the line. An elderly man, who happened to buy one of these
at a local convenience store while they were still warm, told me they reminded him of hot chocolate pudding.
I thought he was kidding until someone else bought one warm and said the same thing.
So, I now recommend that the best time to eat these muffins is, obviously, when they are still warm.*

Preheat oven to 375 degrees F.

½ cup canola oil
3 eggs or equivalent amount of egg substitute
½ cup sugar or equivalent amount of sugar substitute
1 tablespoon vanilla
1½ cups milk
1¾ cups plus 2 tablespoons flour
½ cups plus 2 tablespoons cup cocoa
1 tablespoon baking powder
A pinch of salt (optional)
¾ cup chocolate chips or mini chocolate chips
Additions if desired: ½ cup walnuts, pecans, macadamia nuts, peanuts, peanut butter chips, white chocolate
chips, raisins and/or raspberries. All the additions are optional.

1. Mix together the oil, eggs, sugar, vanilla and milk.

2. Add the dry ingredients and chocolate chips to the egg mixture. Add your choice of an addition last,
   if you are adding any. Mix the batter thoroughly.

3. Grease 4-5 large muffin pan sections or 8-10 regular size muffin pan sections or 18 mini muffin
   pan sections.

4. Fill each muffin section ⅞ full.

5. Bake about 20-40 minutes (depending on the size of muffin sections) or until an inserted knife comes
   out clean. Best eaten within 3 hours of removal from oven.

# Banana Muffins

*Banana muffins come a dime a dozen because of their popularity. But a really good and moist banana muffin is hard to find at high altitude. It took me much trial, effort and a lot of tasting until I had this recipe just right. Since I perfected the recipe, these muffins have been enjoyed by many a customer and friend. Do not try to freeze these muffins, for they do not freeze well at all, although they do stay fresh and moist for a couple of days.*

Preheat oven to 375 degrees F.

6 large, ripe bananas
3 eggs
¾ cup sugar
¾ cups (1½ sticks) butter or margarine (no substitutions)
1 tablespoon vanilla
½ cup milk minus 1 tablespoon
3 cups plus 2 tablespoons flour
1½ teaspoons baking powder
1½ teaspoons baking soda
2 teaspoons cinnamon
**Additions:**
¾ cup chocolate chips, chopped walnuts, peanut butter chips and/or raisins (optional)

1. Mash the bananas in a mixing bowl.

2. Add the eggs, sugar, butter, vanilla and milk to the mashed bananas and mix thoroughly.

3. Add the dry ingredients and choice of an addition and mix batter thoroughly.

4. Grease 8-9 large muffin pan sections or about 14 regular size muffin pan sections or 2 dozen plus mini muffin sections.

5. Fill each muffin section to the top.

6. Bake 20-35 minutes (depending on the size of muffin sections), until muffins feel firm on top or until an inserted knife or toothpick comes out clean.

# Banana Blueberry Muffins

♥

*My oldest girlfriend (who lived in Florida at the time) gave me this recipe when I was whining to her about how baked goods dry out more quickly at high altitude. She told me she got this recipe from a friend and the muffins are super moist. And then she said, "now quit your whining." I proceeded to get off the phone, made a few adjustments for high altitude to the recipe and, yup, she was right. They are truly moist and the taste is great.*

Preheat oven to 350 degrees F.

5 large bananas
2 eggs or equivalent amount of liquid egg substitute
1 cup sugar
1 cup canola oil
2 teaspoons vanilla
¼ cup molasses
3 cups plus 2 tablespoons flour
2 teaspoons baking soda
1 teaspoon baking powder
½ teaspoon cinnamon
1 cup fresh blueberries

1. Mash the bananas in a large mixing bowl.

2. Add the eggs, sugar, oil, vanilla and molasses to the bananas. Mix the egg/banana mixture thoroughly.

3. Add the dry ingredients to the egg/banana mixture and mix.

4. Gently add the blueberries and slowly but thoroughly mix them into the batter.

5. Grease 5-6 large muffin sections or about 1 dozen regular size muffin sections.

6. Fill each section ⅞ full with the batter.

7. Bake about 20-35 minutes (depending on the size of muffin sections) or until an inserted knife or toothpick comes out clean.

Add 1 extra egg when doubling or add 2 extra eggs when tripling this recipe.

*continued on next page*

# Pumpkin Muffins

*I have tasted a variety of muffins in my day, obviously, but when I first tasted this recipe in the form of a loaf of bread, I knew it would be a sure hit as a muffin, too. Moist, spicy and with a speck of butter added prior to devouring, this muffin will make you want to savor every bite.*

Preheat oven to 350 degrees F.

½ cup (1 stick) butter (no substitutions)
1½ cups sugar
2 eggs
1¾ cups flour
1 teaspoon baking soda
1 tablespoon cinnamon
2 teaspoons ginger
½ teaspoon nutmeg
½ teaspoon cloves
⅓ cup ice cold water
1, 16-ounce can plus 2 tablespoons canned pumpkin
½ cup raisins or chopped pecans (optional)

1. Cream together the butter, sugar and eggs.

2. Add the dry ingredients and spices to the egg mixture alternately with the water.

3. Lightly mix the ingredients while slowly adding the pumpkin. Thoroughly mix all the ingredients for 3 minutes on medium speed in the electric mixer.

4. Grease 8-10 large muffin pan sections or 18-24 regular-size muffin pan sections.

5. Fill each muffin section to the top.

6. Bake 40-45 minutes or until an inserted knife or toothpick comes out clean.

# Dad's Favorite Bran Muffins

 SUGAR FREE

*My dad had a heart condition, so he always watched what he ate. Whenever I came into town, he would always lovingly command that I bake him something. About 80 percent of the time I obeyed. One of these commands was to bake him some muffins. So I made him up a batch of these Bran Muffins, and he was quite happy. Although this recipe is similar to other bran muffin recipes, it is much moister and will remain so for two days.*

Preheat oven to 375 degrees F.

2 cups All Bran cereal (no substitutions)
2 cups plus 2 tablespoons milk
⅓ cup canola oil
½ cup sugar or sugar substitute
2 eggs or equivalent amount of liquid egg substitute
1⅓ cups flour
1 tablespoon baking powder
1 tablespoon cinnamon
½ cup or more raisins, walnuts, blueberries or raspberries (optional)

This recipe must be mixed with a rubber spatula, wooden spoon or fork for the best results.

1. Cover cereal completely with milk and let the cereal soak up all the milk. (This takes 10 to 15 minutes.)

2. Add the oil, sugar and eggs to the wet bran and mix thoroughly.

3. Add the remaining ingredients, choice of an addition and gently but thoroughly mix the batter together.

4. Grease 4-5 large muffin sections or about 10-12 regular size muffin sections.

5. Fill each muffin section to the top.

6. Bake 20-35 minutes (depending on the size of muffin sections) or until an inserted toothpick comes out clean but moist.

Add 1 extra egg when doubling or add 2 extra eggs when tripling this recipe.

# Oatmeal Muffins

*This recipe will give you a good and healthy treat to start out the day or to enjoy as an afternoon snack. I wanted a muffin that tasted like oatmeal cookies but just a tad healthier, so once again I played with ingredients. The outcome of my playtime has been enjoyed ever since.*

Preheat oven to 350 degrees F.

TOPPING:
In a separate bowl mix:
½ cup oats
⅓ cup flour
⅓ cup brown sugar or sugar substitute
¼ cup (½ stick) margarine
½ teaspoon cinnamon

Mix all the above ingredients until crumbly and then set aside in a separate bowl.

MUFFINS:
⅓ cup canola oil
2 eggs or equivalent amount of liquid egg substitute
½ cup sugar or sugar substitute
1 cup plus 2 tablespoons oats
1⅔ cups flour
1 tablespoon baking powder
1½ teaspoons cinnamon
½ teaspoon nutmeg
1 cup plus 2 tablespoons milk
½ cup raisins and/or chopped walnuts

1. Thoroughly mix oil, eggs and sugar.

2. Add the remaining ingredients alternately with the milk. Gently but thoroughly mix the batter together.

3. Grease 6 large muffin sections or a dozen regular size muffin sections.

4. Fill the muffin sections almost to the top with the batter and then sprinkle the top each muffin with the crumb topping.

5. Bake 20-30 minutes (depending on the size of muffin sections) or until an inserted toothpick comes out moist but clean.

Add 1 extra egg each time this recipe is doubled.

# Recipe for a Day

Take a little dash of water

And a little leaven of prayer

Add a little bit of morning gold

Dissolved in the morning air

Add some merriment to your meal

And a thought of kith and kin

And then as your prime ingredient

Plenty of work thrown in

Spice it all with the essence of love

Add a little whiff of play

Let a wise old book and a glance above

Complete a well-made day.

# Sweet Breads

\* All recipes can be doubled or tripled.

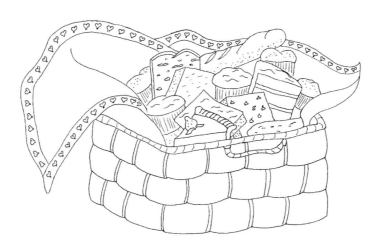

**Clockwise from top:** Pumpkin Bread, Banana Nut Bread, Peach Scones, Philadelphia Sticky Buns

# Banana Bread

---

*The aroma of this bread, while in the oven, will fill your home with a yearning for a slice immediately after it is fully baked. Unfortunately, you will have to wait a minimum of five minutes to let this recipe cool, prior to slicing into it, or you may burn your tongue. I have been baking this recipe for more than 15 years, and to date, nobody has ever refused a piece. Many of my customers also enjoyed this recipe made with chocolate chips.*

Preheat oven to 350 degrees F.

5 large ripe bananas or 6 small bananas
½ cup (1 stick) butter or margarine
½ cup sugar
2 eggs
1⅓ cups flour
¾ teaspoon baking soda
1 teaspoon baking powder
1 tablespoon cinnamon
¾ cup chocolate chips, raisins and/or walnuts (optional)

1. Mash the bananas in a mixing bowl.

2. Add the butter, sugar and eggs to the bananas. Cream the bananas and egg mixture thoroughly.

3. Add the remaining ingredients and mix well.

4. Grease a standard-size bread pan.

5. Pour the batter evenly into the prepared pan.

6. Bake 55-65 minutes or until an inserted knife comes out clean.

# Grandmom's Breakfast Bread

---

*I remember eating this at my Grandmom's when I was a little girl. When I spent the night at her home, she'd always make this recipe for breakfast and serve it with fresh fruit. I never thought it was a special recipe of hers—just that it tasted really good. Then one day, several decades later, I was going through her Tin Box and I found this wonderful recipe! I made it up the next morning and, I swear, I could smell the fabulous scent of the halls in her apartment building where all the elder ladies lived.*

3 beaten eggs
1½ cups milk
½ cup sugar
1 tablespoon vanilla
1½ teaspoons cinnamon and/or nutmeg
8 slices Italian or French bread

1. Thoroughly mix together the eggs, milk, sugar, vanilla and cinnamon and/or nutmeg.

2. Coat each piece of bread with the egg mixture.

3. Fry in oil or butter as you would French toast, until the bread is golden brown on each side.

4. Serve warm with maple syrup, huckleberry syrup or powdered sugar and butter.

# Grandmom's Cinnamon Bread

---

*This recipe tastes as if you had been in the kitchen for hours, instead of just minutes. This is a superb bread to make for a potluck, an unexpected outing, when friends call to say that they are popping in on you in an hour or just for something quick but special. You will never hear a complaint while the last crumb is being gobbled up.*

Preheat oven to 350 degrees F.

STREUSEL:
¼ cup sugar
1¼ tablespoons cinnamon
¼ cup (½ stick) margarine or butter
¾ cup raisins and/or chopped nuts (optional)
Mix above ingredients together and set aside in a separate bowl.

BREAD:
⅓ cup canola oil
¾ cup sugar
3 eggs
1 tablespoon vanilla
2 cups plus 2½ tablespoons flour
1 tablespoon plus 1 teaspoon baking powder
1 cup plus 1 tablespoon buttermilk
2 teaspoons cinnamon

1. Cream together the oil, sugar, eggs and vanilla.

2. Add the remaining ingredients and mix thoroughly.

3. Grease a 9-inch bread pan.

4. Pour half the batter into the pan.

*continued on next page*

5. Sprinkle half the streusel over the bottom layer of batter. Lightly swirl the first streusel layer into the batter.

6. Pour the remaining batter over the streusel and sprinkle the remaining streusel over this layer of batter.

7. With the flat end of a butter knife, lightly swirl the second streusel layer. **Do not mix streusel—swirl!**

8. Bake for 50-60 minutes or until an inserted knife comes out clean.

# Cid's Lemon Poppyseed Bread

*I received many requests to bake poppyseed bread, but at the time the requests began I did not have a recipe. I began asking around for a recipe, when my oldest girlfriend, Cid, said she had an awesome recipe for Lemon Poppyseed Bread. Although, her recipe needed some high-altitude adjustments, when the bread came out of the oven, I knew she was right. This recipe makes a tangy, light and awesome-tasting Lemon Poppyseed Bread. My customers continue to request this recipe today.*

Preheat oven to 350 degrees F.

GLAZE:
½ cup lemon juice
1 cup sugar
Mix and set aside in a separate bowl.

BREAD:
3 eggs
½ cup (1 stick) margarine
1 cup sugar
1 tablespoon lemon curd
3 tablespoons lemon juice
2 teaspoons lemon peel or fresh zest
1½ cups milk
3⅓ cups flour
1½ teaspoons baking powder
⅓ cup poppy seeds

1. Cream together the eggs, butter, sugar, lemon curd, lemon juice, lemon zest and milk.

2. Add the remaining ingredients to the egg mixture. Thoroughly mix together the batter.

3. Grease a 9-inch bread pan.

*continued on next page*

4. Pour the batter into the prepared pan.

5. Bake 1 hour or until an inserted knife comes out clean.

6. Remove from the pan after 5 minutes.

7. Poke holes all over the top of baked loaf with a fork and then, with a pastry brush or with a fork, spread the glaze all over the top of the loaf. You will use every drop of the glaze.

8. Allow to cool for at least 20 minutes prior to slicing to let the glaze soak into the bread.

# Monkey Bread

*This is a marvelous treat to make with young children. While they are breaking the biscuit pieces into smaller pieces and then rolling them in cinnamon sugar, the adult can be cooking the topping. This particular bread looks and tastes as if you and the little ones slaved all day in the kitchen, but in reality, it is as easy to make, as it is to eat.*

Preheat oven to 350 degrees F.

4 tablespoons sugar
2 teaspoons cinnamon
2 cans refrigerated buttermilk biscuits
⅓ cup pecans, walnuts or raisins

1. Mix the cinnamon and sugar together in a large Ziploc bag.

2. Cut each biscuit into 4 pieces and press a few nuts and/or raisins into each biscuit piece.

3. Put the pieces into the plastic baggie with the cinnamon mixture and shake until all pieces are coated.

4. Grease a bundt pan.

5. Place all the cinnamon/sugared biscuit pieces evenly into the prepared bundt pan.

TOPPING:
¾ cup softened butter
¾ cup brown sugar
¼ cup sugar

1. Mix the topping ingredients in a saucepan.

2. Over medium-high heat, boil and stir the ingredients until the mixture comes to a boil.

3. Immediately pour the topping over the biscuit pieces.

*continued on next page*

4. Bake 25-30 minutes or until an inserted knife comes out clean.

5. Immediately remove the bread from the pan by inverting it onto a serving plate. Allow to cool for 5 minutes and enjoy.

# Cranberry Nut Bread

---

*During the autumn and winter seasons, I always get requests to bake this recipe. These requests arrive due to the fact that it is the only time of the year to buy fresh cranberries. Personally, I do not like cranberries, so I have never tasted this bread. But, I have received many, many orders to bake it, which were followed by just as many compliments from its consumers. Some customers ordered two loaves— one for immediate consumption and one for the freezer.*

Preheat oven to 350 degrees F.

½ cup (1 stick) butter or margarine
1 cup sugar
2 eggs
3¼ cups flour
1 tablespoon baking powder
1 teaspoon baking soda
1½ cups pure orange juice
1 teaspoon orange peel or orange zest
3 cups cranberries
¾ cup chopped walnuts (optional)

1. Cream the butter, sugar and eggs.

2. Add the flour, baking powder, baking soda, orange juice and orange peel or zest to the butter mixture.

3. Mix thoroughly while adding the cranberries and walnuts. Mix the batter until all the ingredients are fully incorporated.

4. Grease two 9-inch bread pans.

5. Divide the batter evenly between the prepared pans.

6. Bake 50-60 minutes or until an inserted knife comes out clean.

# Mom's Apple Bread

---

*My Mother used to bake this recipe for "The Ladies" when they would come to her house to play cards.
I happened to walk into such a card game and helped myself to a piece one day, many years ago. I was pretty
impressed, for Mom rarely baked anything from scratch. I proceeded to go into the kitchen,
found her recipe notebook and immediately wrote this recipe down.*

Preheat oven to 350 degrees F.

1 large Granny Smith apple
½ cup (1 stick) butter
1¾ cups plus 2 tablespoons flour
½ cup brown sugar
2 teaspoons baking powder
2 eggs
2 teaspoons cinnamon
½ teaspoon nutmeg
2 ounces cream cheese

1. Grate the Granny Smith apple.

2. Mix the grated apple with the remaining ingredients. Mix all the ingredients together at high speed for 1 minute.

3. Grease a 9-inch bread pan.

4. Pour the batter into the prepared pan.

5. Bake 50-55 minutes or until an inserted knife comes out clean. Allow to cool for 10 minutes prior to serving.

# Blueberry-Orange Bread

♥

*Several years ago, in the middle of the summer, I bought too many fresh blueberries and they were about to go bad. Once again, I turned to my Grandmom's Tin Box to see what blueberry treasures it held. I found an old piece of paper from a magazine page, dated July 1955. On this piece of paper was a woman modeling the fashion of that time. On the back of the page was what turned out to be an amazing blueberry-orange bread recipe.*

Preheat oven to 350 degrees F.

2 eggs or equivalent amount of liquid egg substitute
1 cup milk
½ cup sugar
⅓ cup orange juice
1 tablespoon grated orange peel or fresh orange zest
½ cup canola oil
4½ teaspoons baking powder
¼ teaspoon baking soda
1¼ cups blueberries

1. Cream together the eggs, milk, sugar, orange juice, orange peel and oil.

2. Sift the flour together with the baking powder and baking soda.

3. Add the flour mixture to the egg mixture and mix in thoroughly.

4. Mix 1 tablespoon of extra flour with the blueberries to coat them. Add the blueberries to the batter and gently but thoroughly mix the berries into the batter.

5. Grease a 9-inch bread pan.

6. Pour the batter into the prepared pan.

7. Bake 55-60 minutes or until an inserted knife comes out clean. Allow to cool 15 minutes prior to serving.

# Apricot Nut Bread

*This is a marvelous recipe to bake for someone who loves apricots. I have baked this bread on special request for one person or another since I was in college. This is a wonderful recipe to bake for a Sunday brunch.*

Preheat oven to 350 degrees F.

¼ cup (½ stick) melted margarine
⅓ cup sugar or sugar substitute
2 eggs or equivalent amount of liquid egg substitute
2¼ cups flour
2½ teaspoons baking powder
¼ teaspoon baking soda
1 cup apricot jam or sugar-free apricot jam
½ cup chopped dry apricots, soaked in hot water for 15 minutes to soften
½ cup pure orange juice
½ cup chopped walnuts or pecans

1. Cream together the melted margarine, sugar and eggs.

2. Add the remaining ingredients and mix thoroughly.

3. Grease a 9-inch bread pan.

4. Pour the batter evenly into the prepared pan.

5. Bake 50-60 minutes or until an inserted knife comes out clean. Allow to cool 15-20 minutes prior to serving.

# Cherry Bread

*Almost anything made with cherries tastes good to me, so I played a little and came up with this recipe. Friends and I were gloriously surprised when my playtime results came out of the oven. When I first sliced into the loaf, I noticed one of my friends had his eyes shut. When I questioned him about it, he told me to "shush" and that he was "able to smell the fragrant fields of a cherry orchard." We laughed and proceeded to devour this bread within the next hour.*

Preheat oven to 350 degrees F.

½ cup (1 stick) margarine
2 eggs
½ cup sugar or sugar substitute
½ teaspoon almond extract
2 teaspoons cherry extract
2 cups dark, red pitted cherries, canned or fresh
2¼ cups flour
4 teaspoons baking powder
½ teaspoon baking soda
¼ cup sliced almonds (optional)

1. Cream together the margarine, eggs, sugar, almond extract, cherry extract and cherries until the cherries begin to break into pieces.

2. Add the flour, baking powder and baking soda to the egg mixture.

3. Grease a 9-inch bread pan.

4. Pour the batter into the prepared pan and sprinkle the almond slices on top on top of the batter.

5. Bake 55-60 minutes or until an inserted knife comes out clean. Allow to cool for 15 minutes prior to serving; this bread tastes best when completely cool.

# Cheryl's Zucchini Bread

*Years ago a customer of mine gave me a zucchini that was literally 18 inches long and 6 inches around. I grated it and made a double batch of zucchini muffins, but didn't know what to do with the rest, so I called a friend. She proceeded to give me the following recipe, which has been relished ever since.*

Preheat oven to 350 degrees F.

1 cup canola oil
1¾ cups sugar
½ tablespoon vanilla
⅓ cup molasses
2 eggs or equivalent amount of liquid egg substitute
1 cup grated zucchini
2¼ cups flour
1 teaspoon baking soda
1 tablespoon cinnamon
½ teaspoon nutmeg
1 cup raisins and/or chopped walnuts (optional)

1. Grease a 9-inch bread pan.

2. Mix together the oil, sugar, vanilla, molasses and eggs.

3. Add the grated zucchini to the molasses mixture and mix.

4. Add the remaining ingredients and mix thoroughly for 2 minutes.

5. Pour the batter evenly into the prepared pan.

6. Bake 55-60 minutes or until an inserted knife comes out clean.

# Pumpkin Bread

*The first time I tasted this Pumpkin Bread recipe was prior to a haunted hayride around Halloween.
I never liked pumpkin bread until I tasted this one, and I immediately requested the recipe from the tour guide.
This recipe has an aromatic burst of spice and pumpkin essence, and I was thrilled because I knew
it would stay moist for days. It's the perfect recipe to bake and eat during the autumn season.*

Preheat oven to 350 degrees F.

1 cup (2 sticks) softened butter
4 eggs
3 cups sugar
3 ½ cups flour
2 teaspoons baking soda
⅔ cup ice water
1, 16-ounce can plus 2 tablespoons pumpkin
1 tablespoon cinnamon
2 teaspoons ginger
½ teaspoon nutmeg
½ teaspoon cloves
1 cup raisins and/or chopped nuts (optional)

1. Grease two 9-inch bread pans.

2. Cream together the butter, eggs and sugar.

3. Add the dry ingredients, the spices, raisins and/or chopped nuts and water to the egg mixture alternately with the pumpkin. Thoroughly mix the batter for 2 ½ minutes.

4. Pour the batter evenly into the prepared bread pans.

5. Bake 1 hour or until an an inserted knife comes out clean. Allow to cool 15 minutes prior to serving.

# Grandmom's Nut Bread

*My father was allergic to nuts, so I never tasted this recipe until I found it in my Grandmom's Tin Box. A few days later, I baked this recipe for a friend who enjoys different breads—as long as there aren't any fruits or vegetables added. My friend quickly informed me that he adores this bread.*

Preheat oven to 350 degrees F.

1¾ cups flour
2 teaspoons baking soda
⅓ cup brown sugar
1½ cups oats
1 cup buttermilk
½ cup canola oil
2 eggs
2 teaspoons vanilla
2 teaspoons cinnamon
¾ cup walnuts or pecans, plus a handful extra

1. Grease a 9-inch bread pan.

2. In a mixing bowl, mix together the flour, baking soda, sugar and oats.

3. Add the remaining ingredients to the dry ingredients and mix the batter thoroughly.

4. Pour the batter evenly into the prepared pan.

5. Sprinkle extra nuts on the top of the batter, if you like.

6. Bake 50-55 minutes or until an inserted knife comes out clean. Allow to cool 15-20 minutes prior to serving.

# Scones

*This recipe is so versatile that you can add any fruit, nut or flavored chip to it, and the scones will still taste fabulous. This recipe is not fancy, just simple and pleasantly delightful. Even those who think they do not like scones will enjoy and gobble up the last crumb of this scrumptious treat.*

**8 scones**

Preheat oven to 375 degrees F.

⅓ cup (6 tablespoons) butter or margarine
3 ounces cream cheese
¼ cup sugar
1 teaspoon vanilla
2¼ cups flour
2 teaspoons baking powder
1 egg
½ cup milk minus 1 tablespoon
1 cup blueberries, chopped nuts, dried or fresh fruit and/or mini chocolate chips

1. Cream together the butter, cream cheese, sugar and vanilla.

2. Add the flour, baking powder, egg and milk to the butter mixture and mix.

3. While mixing the ingredients into the batter, add your choice of fruit, nuts, chocolate chips or whatever flavor you desire. (See variations on the next page.) Mix all the ingredients until the dough begins to pull away from the sides of the bowl.

4. Grease a cookie sheet.

5. Remove the dough from the mixing bowl and knead the dough on a floured surface about 10-12 times.

*continued on next page*

6. Pat dough into an 8-10 inch circle and place the dough onto the prepared cookie sheet.

7. With a serrated knife, slice the dough into 8 triangular slices. **Do not separate the slices!**

8. With a pastry brush or fork, brush the dough with a tablespoon of extra milk or water.

9. Bake the scones for 16-18 minutes or until they begin to turn golden.

10. Remove the cookie sheet from the oven and let the scones cool for 4-5 minutes, then separate the slices. Allow to cool for at least 5 more minutes prior to serving after the pieces are separated.

**Variations:**
* For apple scones, add 1 cup diced apples and add 1 teaspoon cinnamon to the dough.
* For lemon scones, omit the vanilla and add 2 teaspoons lemon juice and 1 tablespoon lemon curd to the dough.
* For peach scones, make sure the peaches are diced into small pieces and add them to the dough.

# Philadelphia Sticky Buns

*I truly believe this recipe bakes the best of the best. I remember my Father bringing this treat home
on Sunday mornings when I was a kid. Many years later, he would always have at least a half-dozen fresh rolls
for me at their beach house when I came to visit. I could never find a recipe that was close to the scrumptious
ones I grew up with until I found a taped together, brown piece of newspaper in my Grandmom's Tin Box.
This special piece of newspaper is dated October 1948, and it contains the ingredients and instructions for the
phenomenal recipe below. The first time I made them and they turned out—and it took several tries—
I immediately called a friend of mine who grew up in the same area. I informed her I could smell the ocean,
hear the waves breaking and that I just tasted a bit of heaven. She came right over, tasted these sticky buns and
immediately agreed that we had died, gone to the beach and then landed in heaven.*

Please, do not try this recipe when the humidity level is below 85 percent. The taste will be there, but the
height won't. You need a lot of humidity in the atmosphere for this recipe to turn out just right. However,
if you just can't wait for a humid day, go for it anyway—I have.

**16-18 rolls**

1 package dry yeast
½ cup warm water
1⅓ cups lukewarm milk
1 tablespoon sugar
5¼ cups flour
½ cup butter, margarine or Crisco
¾ cup sugar
1½ cup raisins and/or chopped walnuts or pecans
2¼ cups brown sugar
2 eggs
32 ounces light corn syrup
⅔ cups cinnamon
⅓ cup molasses
1 stick butter, soft

*continued on next page*

1. In a large cup, sprinkle the yeast over the warm water; cover and let sit undisturbed for 10 minutes.

2. Heat the milk until lukewarm and add 1 tablespoon sugar to the milk.

3. After stirring the yeast mixture to be sure every grain is blended and smooth, stir the yeast mixture into the milk.

4. Measure out 2¼ cups flour and place into a large mixing bowl. Pour the yeast mixture into the center of the flour and mix from the center out until the mixture barely jiggles; cover and set aside.

5. In a small mixing bowl, beat ½ cup butter, margarine or Crisco until light. Add the ¾ cup sugar and the 2 eggs (add 1 egg at a time and beat thoroughly after each addition).

6. When the yeast mixture is looking light and bubbly, add the sugar mixture (a big spoonful at a time) and mix into the dough after each addition. Beat the yeast mixture well.

7. Gradually, at slow speed, add 3 cups flour to the yeast mixture. Mix the dough for 2-3 minutes at a slow speed until all ingredients are fully incorporated.

8. Cover the dough and let it rise in a warm spot until double in bulk; this will take a couple of hours. (Do not place the bowl on direct heat such as an oven or fireplace.)

9. Once the dough has doubled in bulk, prepare the pans. I use two 10x2-inch round pans or 3, 9x2-inch pans. Butter (only use butter) each pan generously and completely over the bottom and up the sides. Pour light corn syrup into each buttered pan until each pan is a ¼-inch full of the syrup. If you like, lightly sprinkle the syrup with raisins and/or chopped walnuts or pecans. (About ½ cup raisins or nuts.) Set pans aside.

10. Take about one-third of the dough and, on a floured surface, roll it out into a rectangle about ¼-inch thick.

11. Spread this one-third of the dough with one-third of the stick of soft butter. Thickly sprinkle ¾ cup brown sugar on top of the butter. Then, sprinkle 2 tablespoons cinnamon on top of the brown sugar. Cover the cinnamon with ½ cup raisins and/or chopped nuts. Drizzle 2 tablespoons of the molasses over the cinnamon and raisins and/or nuts. Avoid clumps of molasses when drizzling it.

12. Roll up the one-third of prepared dough tightly, like a jellyroll.

13. With a floured knife, cut the rolled-up dough into 1½-inch thick slices.

14. Place the rolls with cut sides down into the pans prepared. Make sure the rolls do not touch each other and that the pan is not overcrowded.

15. Repeat this procedure with the remaining dough.

16. Cover the pans and let the rolls rise until double in bulk, about 2 hours.

17. Uncover the pans.

18. Preheat oven to 350 degrees F.

19. Bake the rolls until golden brown on top or when an inserted toothpick comes out relatively clean, about 20-30 minutes.

20. When the rolls are fully baked, remove the pans from the oven and immediately invert the pans onto plates or a serving tray lined with waxed paper. If you cannot wait, stick a fork into one roll and immediately taste it, but be careful not to burn your tongue.

Store the sticky buns in an airtight container or on a plate covered with waxed paper and then covered with tightly fitted cellophane. If wrapping the buns to take somewhere, make sure the top is first covered with waxed paper, then wrapped in cellophane or put in an airtight container.

# Bubba's Easy Cinnamon Rolls

*I got this cinnamon roll recipe from an elderly woman who lived in Kentucky. I first tasted them at her home and immediately requested the recipe. She was so flattered that she wrote the recipe down for me on the spot. She said she never thought they were anything special until I informed her otherwise.*

**12 plus rolls**

1 cup sugar
3 tablespoons cinnamon
Mix together and set aside in a small bowl.

¼ cup (½ stick) melted butter, set aside
1 package dry yeast
¼ cup warm water
2 eggs
3 tablespoons sugar
⅛ teaspoon baking soda
2½ tablespoons butter or margarine
3¼ cups plus 1 tablespoon flour

1. Mix together the yeast and the warm water and set aside for 5-7 minutes.

2. Add the eggs, sugar, baking soda and the 2½ tablespoons butter to the yeast and mix together.

3. Gradually add the flour to the yeast mixture and continue mixing the dough thoroughly.

4. Lightly flour a flat surface.

5. Remove the dough from the mixing bowl, place on the floured surface and knead the dough for 2 minutes.

6. Cover and let the dough relax for 10-15 minutes.

7. Take half the dough and roll it into a rectangle about ¼-inch thick.

8. With a pastry brush or fork, brush the dough with half the melted butter. Sprinkle half the cinnamon sugar on top of the butter. Sprinkle half the raisins and/or nuts on top of the cinnamon sugar.

9. Roll up tightly like a jellyroll and pinch seams together to seal.

10. Repeat this procedure with the remaining dough.

11. Heavily butter the bottom and up the sides of two 9x9-inch cake pans.

12. Slice each roll into 1½-inch pieces; divide rolls evenly among each pan, placing them in the prepared pans, cut sides up.

13. Cover each pan and let the rolls rise in a warm, cozy place until double in bulk, about 1-1½ hours.

14. Preheat oven to 375 degrees F.

15. Bake rolls about 15-20 minutes, until golden and an inserted toothpick comes out clean.

16. Prepare the Powdered Sugar Frosting (according to the recipe below) while the rolls are baking.

17. Remove the pans from the oven. While still warm, spread the rolls with the Powdered Sugar Frosting.

POWDERED SUGAR FROSTING:
(Double this recipe if you like a lot of icing on your cinnamon rolls.)
1 cup sifted powdered sugar
2-2½ tablespoons milk
½ teaspoon vanilla
Mix all ingredients together.

# Recipe for Living

*I was given this recipe when I was going through a major medical disorder called Acromegaly. I passed this recipe onto my Father when he was very ill and it made him smile. This special recipe helped us make it through every day, whether we were healthy or not. I hope this recipe helps you make it through every day as well.*

1 cup love
¼ cup firmly packed will power
3 ounces determination
A dash of flexibility
1 large head understanding
A few leaves awareness (fresh, if possible)
½ pound pride, cut into small portions
1 pound humility
A sprinkling of common sense
A pinch of adventure
1 full (8 ounce) can foresight
A hint of hindsight
A few sprigs of humor
Season to taste

Sauté Love and Understanding until tender.
Mix well and continue gently cooking.
In a large bowl, blend will power and determination well to avoid procrastination, adding a dash of flexibility to accommodate life's delicate variations. Fold in the few leaves of awareness (more, if you savor knowledge).
Set aside to rise and expand in flavor throughout the days.
In a separate bowl, combine pride, whisked lightly with humility.
Pour in common sense and sprinkle lightly with adventure.
Set oven with foresight for each new day, but hindsight just enough to profit from the old. Season entire mixture with humor.
Bake for 24 hours, testing often and adjusting to the wonders of each new day.

# Fruit-Filled Treats

---

*\* All the following recipes can be frozen for up to eight days without affecting the taste or texture.*
*\* To reheat most of the following recipes, either scoop out a desired individual amount and heat*
*in the microwave, or place a piece of foil over the entire pan or dish and reheat*
*at the original baking temperature for 10 to 15 minutes.*
*\* All fruit-filled recipes prepared in a 9x13-inch pan can be cut into nine, 12 or 16 pieces.*
*All dishes prepared in a casserole dish will serve six to eight people.*

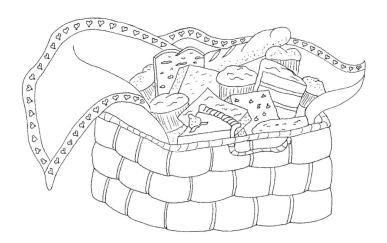

# Clare's Favorite Lemon Bars

---

*I named this recipe after Clare, for she is the biggest fan of these treats I know. Many years ago, just before Christmas, I always received a box of goodies in the mail from my dear friend, Patt. The box always contained Lemon Bars, and they were always the first treat I consumed. When I first began baking for a living, I requested her Lemon Bar recipe, of course. She informed me that it was her Mother's recipe, but she gave it to me anyway. Since then it has been requested and enjoyed by many, but by none as much as Clare.*

Preheat oven to 350 degrees F.

1 box Betty Crocker's Super Moist Lemon Cake mix
1 egg
⅓ cup (¾ stick) melted margarine
2 eggs
1 cup sugar
¼ cup fresh lemon juice
2 teaspoons grated lemon peel or zest
¼ teaspoon baking powder
2 tablespoons powdered sugar, set aside

1. Mix the box of cake mix, 1 egg and melted margarine until crumbly. Reserve 1 cup of the cake crumbs for later. (I usually get the crumbs from the bottom of the mixing bowl where the ingredients have a tendency to settle.)

2. Grease a 9x13-inch pan.

3. Firmly press the remaining crumbs onto the bottom of the pan.

4. Bake the crust until it begins to turn light brown, about 13-15 minutes.

5. While baking the crust, prepare the filling.

*continued on next page*

FILLING:

With a fork, thoroughly mix together the 2 eggs, sugar, lemon juice, lemon peel and baking powder.

6. Remove the crust from the oven.

7. Pour the filling evenly onto the hot crust.

8. Sprinkle reserved crumbs evenly over the filling.

9. Bake another 15 minutes or until crumbs begin to turn light brown.

10. Remove the pan from the oven; cool for 10-15 minutes and sprinkle with the powdered sugar. Allow to cool completely prior to cutting. Wrap the pan in cellophane or cut and individually wrap 12-16 bars.

# Blueberry and Raspberry Fruit Bars

*As always, when I visited my folks, my Dad would affectionately command that I bake him something.
As he got older, he developed a heart condition and diabetes, so fulfilling this command was not an easy task.
During one such visit, after his love-filled command, I proceeded to call his doctor to get an idea of what fruits
he could and could not eat. The doctor informed me that he could have blueberries and raspberries, for they
have low sugar content. As an outcome of this telephone conversation, I lovingly developed the following
recipe. From the first time this recipe came out of the oven until he passed away, whenever
I visited my parents I was summoned to bake two batches of this recipe. One batch was
for while I was visiting and the other batch was for the freezer.*

Preheat oven to 350 degrees F.

1½ cups (3 sticks) melted margarine or canola oil
3 cups plus 2 tablespoons oats
2⅔ cups flour
¾ cup brown sugar or brown sugar substitute
1½ teaspoons cinnamon
4 cups blueberries, fresh or frozen, thawed and drained of juice
2 cups raspberries, fresh or frozen, thawed and drained of juice
1 cup raspberry jam (sugar-free jam works fine)
1½ tablespoons flour

1. Mix together the margarine, oats, 2⅔ cups flour, sugar and cinnamon until ingredients hold together
   and crumbs begin to form. The dough will be somewhat moist.

2. Reserve 1¼ cups of crumbs from the bottom of the mixing bowl in a small bowl and set aside to use for
   the topping.

3. Grease a 9x13-inch pan.

4. Evenly press the crumbs onto the bottom of the prepared pan.

*continued on next page*

5. Bake bottom crust for 20 minutes.

6. While baking the crust, prepare the filling.

FILLING:
In a medium bowl, place the blueberries, raspberries, jam and 1½ tablespoons of flour. Gently mix until the jam is thoroughly incorporated.

7. Remove the crust from the oven and immediately spread filling evenly and completely over crust.

8. Remix the reserved crumbs, to further break them up, and sprinkle the crumbs over the filling.

9. Bake another 20 minutes. Allow to cool completely prior to serving.

Cut into 9, 12 or 16 pieces and cover the pan in cellophane.

**Variations:**
* Raspberry jam with blackberries.
* Apricot jam with peaches.
* Blueberry jam with blackberries or any combination of the fruits given.
Note that strawberries get too mushy in this recipe.

# Cherry Peach Crisp

 **SUGAR** FREE

*This is one of my favorite recipes. I often make it for myself for dinner on a cold winter night, when I don't feel like eating veggies, meat, poultry or fish. It is, however, a simple, fulfilling and healthy treat anytime of day. For an extra special treat, serve it hot with a dollop of vanilla ice cream, or my choice, coffee ice cream. I have made this recipe sugar-free for myself and friends before, and no one knew it was sugar-free. I will always refer to this recipe as comfort food—and as just what the doctor ordered.*

Preheat oven to 350 degrees F.

1 cup juice from canned or frozen and thawed dark, red cherries
2½ tablespoons minute tapioca
Stir the cherry juice and the tapioca together in a small bowl; cover and let sit for 15 minutes.

½ cup (1 stick) melted margarine or canola oil
1 cup plus 2 tablespoons flour
1 cup plus 2 tablespoons oats
¼ teaspoon baking soda
¼ teaspoon baking powder
⅔ cup brown sugar or brown sugar substitute
2 teaspoons cinnamon
4½ cups dark, red cherries
2 cups sliced peaches, fresh and peeled or canned in light syrup and drained of syrup

1. Gently, with a fork or in a mixer, mix together the margarine, oats, flour, baking soda, baking powder and cinnamon until ingredients begin to hold together and crumbs begin to form. (Do not over mix). Reserve 1⅓ cups crumbs from the bottom of the bowl and set aside.

2. Grease a 9x13-inch pan.

3. Press the remaining crumbs firmly into the bottom of the prepared pan.

4. Cover the bottom crust evenly with the cherries.

*continued on next page*

5. Fill any bald spaces on the crust with all the sliced peaches. (Overlapping of fruits is fine, for you want the entire bottom crust covered with the fruit.)

6. Lightly and evenly trickle the tapioca/juice mixture over the fruit.

7. Beat the reserved crumbs in a mixer or with a fork to break them up into smaller crumbs. Sprinkle the crumbs evenly over the fruit.

8. Bake about 35 minutes or until you begin to see the fruit bubbling. This tastes best when served 10 minutes out of the oven. Store leftovers in the refrigerator and reheat to serve.

# Peach Pecan Crisp

*Simple, easy and delicious, this recipe is sure to impress all to whom you serve it. For many generations, there has been a difference of opinion over what is a pie versus a cobbler or a crisp. Addressing this question with a member of an elder generation could be difficult, but I put it this way: Pie has a thin crust; cobbler has a thicker, biscuit-type crust; and a crisp has a sweeter, crispier crust with a tad of brown sugar added to it. Just my opinion.*

Preheat oven to 375 degrees F.

TOPPING:
1 cup flour
⅓ cup firmly packed brown sugar
1 tablespoon plus 1 teaspoon sugar
1 teaspoon cinnamon
¼ teaspoon nutmeg
⅓ cup cold butter, chopped
½ cup chopped pecans

1. Mix the flour, sugars and spices with a pastry blender or a wire beater in an electric mixer.

2. Add the cold butter to the flour mixture and mix.

3. When mixture begins to slightly hold together but is still crumbly, add the chopped pecans and blend them into the flour mixture.

4. Set the mixture aside in a smaller bowl.

FILLING:
8 cups sliced peaches, fresh and peeled or canned light peaches, drained of syrup
1½ tablespoons flour
1 tablespoon sugar
¼ teaspoon nutmeg

*continued on next page*

1. Mix the peaches lightly with the flour, sugar and nutmeg.

2. Grease a deep dish pie plate, an 8-inch square pan or a 3-quart casserole dish.

3. Place the peaches into your choice of dish.

4. Sprinkle the peaches evenly with the topping.

5. Bake about 40 minutes or until topping is golden brown and peach juices are bubbly. (If the topping begins to brown before juices begin to bubble, place a sheet of foil over the topping to prevent burning and continue baking.)

Store any leftovers in the refrigerator and reheat at the original baking temperature.

# Grandmom's Peach Cobbler

*My Grandmom did not make peach pie often—instead, she made peach cobbler. Whenever I would bake this recipe for friends or customers, they always raved about how fabulous it tasted. Full of peaches, with just the right amount of spice, this makes a treat your family will request over and over again.*

Preheat oven to 375 degrees F.

FILLING:
In a dish place:
4 cups peeled and sliced peaches or light canned and sliced peaches drained of syrup
¾ cup sugar or sugar substitute
1 teaspoon cinnamon
¼ teaspoon nutmeg
1 tablespoon fresh lemon juice
¼ cup (½ stick) cold butter, sliced

1. Well-grease a 2-quart casserole dish.

2. Combine the sugar, cinnamon, nutmeg and juice.

3. Gently, with a fork or spoon, mix the sugar and spices in with the peaches.

4. Place the peaches into the prepared dish and dot them with the sliced butter.

5. Set the peaches aside and prepare the topping.

TOPPING:
1 cup plus 2 tablespoons flour
1 teaspoon cinnamon
¼ teaspoon nutmeg
2 tablespoons sugar
2 teaspoons baking powder

*continued on next page*

¼ cup (½ stick) cold butter, sliced into little pieces
⅓ cup plus 1 tablespoon milk

1. Use a pastry blender, wire beater or 2 knives to mix all the dry ingredients together. Add the cold butter.

2. Gradually add the milk and mix the ingredients with a fork.

3. Gather the dough together and place on a lightly floured surface.

4. Knead the dough about 10 times or until smooth.

5. Shape dough to fit a casserole dish, but not more than about ½-inch thick.

6. Place the dough over the fruit and press down on the fruit along the edges of the dish as if tucking the fruit into the dish. Trim away any excess dough.

7. Bake 40-50 minutes or until juices begin to bubble and the fruit feels tender when pierced through the dough with a knife or fork. (If the topping begins to brown before juices begin to bubble, place a sheet of foil over the topping to prevent burning and continue baking.)

To reheat, cover the dish with foil and heat at the original baking temperature for 10 minutes or dish out the desired amount onto a plate and microwave.

# Cherry Cobbler

*This recipe makes a great dessert to serve on a cold and rainy summer evening. I prefer to use fresh dark, red cherries. The cherries must be pitted, so have the children pit the cherries while you are preparing the topping. The kids will get a kick out of helping, and they will be thrilled when gulping down the result of their hard work. This treat looks outstanding on a Fourth of July picnic table.*

Preheat oven to 375 degrees F.

TOPPING:
1 cup plus 2 tablespoons flour
1 teaspoon cinnamon
3 tablespoons sugar
2 teaspoons baking powder
¼ cup (½ stick) cold butter sliced into little pieces
⅓ cup plus 1 tablespoon milk
¼ cup sliced almonds (optional)

1. Use a pastry blender, wire beater or 2 knives to mix all the dry ingredients together. Add the cold butter.

2. Gradually add the milk and mix the ingredients with a fork until it begins to hold together.

3. Gather the dough together and place on a lightly floured surface.

4. Knead the dough about 10 times or until smooth.

5. Shape dough to fit a casserole dish, but not more than about ½-inch thick.

*continued on next page*

FILLING:

4 cups fresh pitted dark, red cherries, or frozen or canned dark, red cherries, drained of juice

¾ cup sugar or sugar substitute

1 teaspoon cinnamon

1 teaspoon almond extract

1 tablespoon fresh lemon juice

¼ cup (½ stick) cold butter, sliced

1. Grease a 3-quart casserole dish.

2. Place the cherries into the prepared dish.

3. Combine the sugar, cinnamon, almond extract and lemon juice, and with a fork or spoon, gently mix into the cherries.

4. Dot the cherries with the sliced butter. Set the cherries aside.

5. Place the topping (dough) over the filling and press down along the edges of the dish as if tucking the fruit into the dish. Trim away any excess dough.

6. Sprinkle sliced almonds on top of the dough.

7. Bake 40-50 minutes or until the juices begin to bubble and the fruit is tender when pierced through the dough with a knife or fork. (If the topping begins to brown before juices begin to bubble, place a sheet of foil over the topping to prevent burning and continue baking.)

To reheat, cover the dish with foil and heat at the original baking temperature for 10 minutes or dish out the desired amount onto a plate and microwave.

# Healthy Cherry Cobbler

*Frequently, I received requests for healthy baked goods. Due to a personal mission to try to meet most of my customers' dietary needs, I came up with the following recipe. One of my customers from the city requested anything made with fruit and oats, and about once a month she specifically requested this cobbler.*

Preheat oven to 375 degrees F.

2½ bags frozen and thawed or 3 cans dark, red cherries
2½ tablespoons minute tapioca (only if using frozen cherries)
½ cup sugar or ½ cup sugar substitute
½ teaspoon almond extract

1. Grease a 3-quart casserole dish.

2. Mix the cherries and the tapioca in the prepared dish, cover and then let the mixture rest for 20 minutes.

3. Pour the sugar and almond extract over the cherries and lightly toss together.

4. Set the dish of sugared cherries aside and prepare the topping.

TOPPING:
1¼ cups oats
1¼ cups flour
1 teaspoon cinnamon
⅓ cup canola oil
¼ cup sliced almonds (optional)
½ cup skim milk
2 tablespoons sliced almonds (optional)

1. Mix together the oats, flour, cinnamon, oil and half the almonds until coarse crumbs begin to form.

2. Add the milk to the crumbs and mix until crumbs are moist.

*continued on next page*

3. Using a medium to large spoon, drop the crumb mixture by spoonsful onto the cherries until there are no crumbs left.

4. Sprinkle the top of the crumbs with the sliced almonds.

5. Bake 25-35 minutes or until golden brown.

To reheat, cover the dish with foil and heat at the original baking temperature for 10 minutes or dish out the desired amount onto a plate and microwave.

# Cherry Brown Betty

*While searching for more recipes in my Grandmom's Tin Box, I came across a page from a magazine that was dated 1952. I was reading the page when I recognized the ingredients and remembered that she would make me this recipe and I would call it, "the cherry stuff." I rapidly made the recipe after finding it, and it tasted just as good as when I was a little girl. I continue to make it today when I am feeling homesick and it's chilly outside. I added a handful of almonds, and now I describe this recipe as "the really good cherry stuff."*

Preheat oven to 375 degrees F.

2 ½ cups canned or frozen and thawed, sour or dark, red cherries (I prefer dark, red cherries.)
Drain the juice into a cup or small bowl.

2 teaspoons lemon juice
¾ cup cherry juice, drained from the fruit
3 cups soft bread crumbs or 6-6 ½ slices of fresh bread (Break bread into crumbs by holding onto a slice of bread and tearing crumbs away with a fork.)
¼ cup (½ stick) melted butter
½ cup sugar or sugar substitute
1 teaspoon lemon peel or fresh grated lemon zest
3 tablespoons sliced almond pieces
¾ teaspoon cinnamon

1. Grease a 2–3 quart casserole dish.

2. Mix together the lemon juice and the cherry juice and set aside.

3. Put all the bread crumbs into a medium-large bowl.

4. Gradually pour the melted butter over the crumbs while tossing the crumbs with a fork.

5. Add the sugar, lemon peel, almonds and cinnamon to the bread crumbs. Mix well with a fork.

6. Mix the cherries into the bread crumbs.

*continued on next page*

7. Pour the cherry mixture into the prepared dish.

8. Slowly and evenly pour the cherry/lemon juice over the cherries and bread crumbs.

9. Bake 20-25 minutes. Serve hot or warm with ice cream or table cream, if you prefer.

To reheat, cover the dish with foil and heat at the original baking temperature for 10 minutes or dish out the desired amount onto a plate and heat in the microwave.

# Apple Brown Betty

*I found this recipe in my Grandmom's Tin Box, although I do not know to whom it belonged.*
*It was not in handwriting that I recognized. Nevertheless, I tried it, changed some of the*
*initial ingredients, and the result is unbelievably scrumptious.*

Preheat oven to 350 degrees F.

1½ cups sugar or 1⅓ cup sugar substitute
2 teaspoons cinnamon
½ teaspoon nutmeg
Mix together the sugar, cinnamon and nutmeg and set aside.

5 red or golden apples, peeled and sliced into ⅓-½ inch slices
2 cups bread crumbs
½ cup (1 stick) melted margarine or butter
4 tablespoons fresh orange juice
2 tablespoons water

1. Grease a 3-quart casserole dish completely with butter or margarine.

2. Mix together the juice and water and set aside.

3. Layer half the apples, then half the bread crumbs, half the cinnamon/sugar and half the melted margarine.

4. Then, lightly distribute half the water/juice over the bottom half of the apples.

5. Repeat this layering process with the remaining ingredients for the second layer.

6. Cover the apples and the dish with a casserole lid or foil.

7. Bake for 40-50 minutes or until the apples are tender when pierced with a knife or fork. Serve as is or with ice cream or table cream.

*continued on next page*

To reheat, cover the dish with foil and heat at the original baking temperature for 10 minutes or dish out the desired amount onto a plate and microwave.

# Cheddar Apple Crisp

*Cheddar cheese and apples are one of the oldest but tastiest combinations to mankind.*
*They're a great combination for a great treat. This crisp is superb on a cool autumn evening.*

Preheat oven to 350 degrees F.

8 red or golden apples, peeled and thinly sliced
A few drops lemon juice
Sprinkle the lemon juice over the apples and set aside.

¼ cup water
¼ cup brown sugar
2½ tablespoons flour
¾ teaspoon cinnamon
¼ teaspoon nutmeg
1½ cups grated cheddar cheese
1 cup plus 1 tablespoon oats
¼ cup firmly packed brown sugar
¼ cup (½ stick) melted margarine or butter
½ cup grated cheddar cheese

1. Grease a 3-quart casserole dish.

2. Mix the water, sugar, flour, spices and 1½ cups cheese with the apples and set aside in the prepared dish.

3. Mix together the oats, brown sugar, melted butter and ½ cup cheese until fairly crumbly.

4. Sprinkle the oat crumbs over the apples.

5. Bake 30-40 minutes or until the apples are tender when pierced with a knife or fork.

To reheat, cover the dish with foil and heat at the original baking temperature for 10 minutes or dish out the desired amount onto a plate and microwave.

# Apple Cranberry Crisp

**SUGAR** FREE

*This is an outstanding treat to make when fresh cranberries are in season. The combination of apples and cranberries will fill your home with an irresistible aroma that will have everyone impatient until this crisp comes out of the oven. Serve warm with vanilla or cinnamon ice cream for the best flavor.*

Preheat oven to 350 degrees F.

2 cups or 4 granny smith apples, peeled and thinly sliced
2 cups fresh cranberries
2 teaspoons fresh lemon juice
1 teaspoon cinnamon
3 tablespoons brown sugar or brown sugar substitute

TOPPING:
⅓ cup flour
¼ cup firmly packed brown sugar or brown sugar substitute
¼ cup sugar or sugar substitute
¾ teaspoon cinnamon
¼ teaspoon nutmeg
⅓ cup (¾ stick) cold butter or margarine, sliced into pieces

1. Completely butter a 3-quart casserole dish.

2. Place sliced apples and cranberries into the prepared dish and toss the fruit with the lemon juice, cinnamon and 3 tablespoons brown sugar.

3. Put casserole dish aside and prepare the topping.

TOPPING:

1. Mix together the flour, sugars, spices and butter.

2. Spread the flour mixture over the fruit and lightly press down with the palm of your hand to even the dough out.

3. Bake 45-55 minutes or until the fruit is tender when pierced with a knife or fork.

To reheat, cover the dish with foil and heat at the original baking temperature for 10 minutes or dish out the desired amount onto a plate and microwave.

# Caramel Apple Bars

*This recipe makes a pleasant treat to have waiting for your children when they come home from school. These sweet bars slightly resemble caramel apples, just a tad healthier, and they will not break any teeth while biting into the treat. These make remarkable snacks to take with you when you are on the run or to pack in the children's lunch box for a snack.*

Preheat oven to 350 degrees F.

2½-3 cups or 5 large Granny Smith apples, peeled and thinly sliced
2 tablespoons fresh lemon juice
1 teaspoon cinnamon (optional)
2 cups flour
2 cups oats
¾ cup firmly packed brown sugar
1 teaspoon baking soda
½ cup chopped walnuts or pecans (optional)
1¼ cups (2½ sticks) melted margarine or butter

24-26 caramels, unwrapped
1, 14-ounce can sweetened condensed milk
¼ cup (½ stick) margarine or butter
1 teaspoon vanilla

1. Grease a 9x13-inch pan.

2. Sprinkle apples with lemon juice and cinnamon, mix and set aside.

3. Mix together the flour, oats, sugar, baking soda, nuts and margarine until the mixture begins to hold together but is still crumbly. In a small bowl, reserve 1¼ cups of the crumbs from the bottom of the mixing bowl.

4. Press the remaining crumbs over the bottom of the prepared pan, making sure the entire bottom of the pan is covered.

5. Bake the crust for about 10 minutes.

6. While baking the bottom crust, prepare the caramel topping.

CARAMEL TOPPING:

1. In a saucepan over low heat, stir the caramels, condensed milk, butter and vanilla until all the caramels are fully melted.

2. Remove the crust pan from the oven and place the apples on the hot, baked crust.

3. Pour the caramel mixture evenly over the apples.

4. Remix the reserved crumbs to break them up. Sprinkle the crumbs over the caramel and apples.

5. Bake 20-25 minutes or until caramel begins to bubble. Cool completely and cut into 12-16 bars; keep the pan or individual pieces wrapped in cellophane for freshness.

# Blueberry Cream Cheese Crumb Bars

*According to my Mother, these are one of the best baked goods I ever made for her and "The Ladies."*
*All I can say is, after making them at my parent's home, I left the house and came back about five hours later*
*to discover that the entire pan was gone. I thought they might have turned out awful and were thrown out.*
*When I asked my Mom, she said they were wonderful and, upon request, she sent some home with*
*my Aunts and neighbors, so they could share them with their families.*

Preheat oven to 350 degrees F.

2½ cups flour
1⅓ cups sugar
¾ cup butter or margarine
¾ cup milk
2 eggs
2 teaspoons baking powder

2 cups fresh blueberries

2 teaspoons vanilla
1 8-ounce package cream cheese
2 tablespoons sugar

2 teaspoons cinnamon
⅓ cup brown sugar
½ cup chopped walnuts

1. Grease a 9x13-inch pan.

2. Mix the flour, sugar, butter, milk, eggs and baking powder together.

3. Spread the flour mixture (the crust) evenly into the prepared pan.

4. Spread the fresh blueberries on top of the crust.

5. Thoroughly mix the vanilla, cream cheese and sugars.

6. Gently spread the cream cheese mixture over the blueberries.

7. Mix the cinnamon, sugar and walnuts together. Sprinkle the cinnamon/sugar evenly over the cream cheese and blueberries.

8. Bake 35-40 minutes or until the topping is golden but not brown or until an inserted knife comes out clean. Allow to cool completely prior to cutting into bars.

**Variation:**
Substitute the blueberries with fresh raspberries, blackberries or huckleberries.

# Kitchen Fun

Serve a laugh with meatloaf

Serve a smile with a steak

Serve a grin with gingerbread

And chuckles with a cake

Whistle with the waffles

Sing a song with salad

Hum a tune while kneading bread

Don't you know a ballad?

Beat time with a rolling pin

Tap dance while you fry,

There's kitchen fun for everyone

Who'll make it—why not try?

# Brownies and Such

*\* Each of these recipes can be frozen for up to five days.*
*\* Each of these recipes can be cut into nine, 12 or 16 pieces.*
*\* Always keep covered, even after cutting into pieces.*

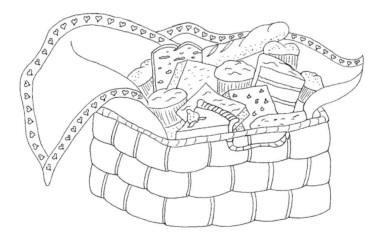

**Clockwise from top:** Chocolate Fudge Brownies, Patt's Favorite White Chocolate Brownies, Oreo Crumb Cheesecake Bars

# Chocolate Fudge Brownies

---

*It took me a little over two months to come up with this recipe. I wanted a homemade brownie baked from scratch that tasted similar to the original Duncan Hines Brownie my Mom used to bake. So I played. I tried sweetened chocolate and unsweetened chocolate squares, 1 pound of butter, 1 cup of butter, etc., etc. Then one morning around 3 a.m. the following came out of the oven. I tasted them once, then twice and then woke up my ex to taste them. He tasted them and said, "You did it, these are great. What did you do?" I looked at him and said "uh oh". Then, I went back to the prep table with a piece of paper and a pen, shut my eyes and wrote down the recipe. These brownies are so rich and wonderful, I'm sure whoever you bake them for will think so too.*

Preheat oven to 350 degrees F.

1½ cups (3 sticks) melted butter
3 cups sugar
6 large eggs, if using smaller eggs, use 7 instead of 6
1 tablespoon vanilla
1 cup plus 1½ tablespoons European or Dutch cocoa (You can use regular cocoa, but the brownies will not be as dark or rich.)
Scant 2 cups flour
1 teaspoon baking soda
1 cup chocolate chips

1. Cream together the butter, sugar, eggs and vanilla for 3 minutes.

2. Add the cocoa to the butter mixture and thoroughly mix for 1 minute.

3. Add the flour, baking powder and chocolate chips to the mixture and thoroughly mix for 2 more minutes.

4. Grease a 9x13-inch pan.

5. Pour the batter evenly into the prepared pan.

6. Bake 40-50 minutes or until an inserted knife or toothpick comes out clean. (The center will fall just a tad.)

When **tripling** this recipe, add 1 extra egg, but not when making a double batch.

# Raspberry or Cherry Fudge Brownies

*Al, who enjoyed anything made with raspberries, was a regular customer of mine. One summer day, when an abundance of berries was available at a decent price, he suggested I try adding raspberries to my brownies. So I did, and I brought samples to him and some other customers. They thought they were awesome. I thought of adding the cherries after I pitted too many one rainy summer morning, and they tasted great, too. Thus, for a bit of an alternative to the fudge brownie, add some raspberries or cherries.*

Preheat oven to 350 degrees F.

1½ cups (3 sticks) melted butter
3 cups sugar
6 large eggs, if using smaller eggs, use 7 instead of 6
1 tablespoon vanilla
1 cup plus 1½ tablespoons European or Dutch Cocoa (You can use regular cocoa, but the brownies will not
   be as dark or rich.)
2 cups flour
1 teaspoon baking soda
1 cup chocolate chips
1½ cups fresh raspberries or pitted cherries

1. Cream together the butter, sugar, eggs and vanilla for 3 minutes.

2. Add the cocoa to the butter mixture and thoroughly mix for 1 minute.

3. Add the flour, baking powder and chocolate chips to the mixture and thoroughly mix for 2 more minutes.

4. Gently fold the raspberries or cherries thoroughly into the batter.

5. Grease a 9x13-inch pan.

6. Pour the batter into the prepared pan.

7. Bake 45-55 minutes or until an inserted knife or toothpick comes out clean. (The center will fall just a tad.)

When **tripling** this recipe, add 1 extra egg, but not when making a double batch.

# Chocolate Caramel Pecan Brownies

*Due to a fact that I know many people who enjoy eating Chocolate Turtle candy,*
*I came up with the following recipe because I thought it would be fun and taste good, too.*
*My Mom loved them, and so did my vet and her assistant. Not too gooey, just right.*

Preheat oven to 350 degrees F.

1 cup (2 sticks) melted butter
2 cups sugar
2 eggs
1 tablespoon vanilla
1¼ cups flour
¾ cup European or Dutch cocoa (You can use regular cocoa, but the brownies
   will not be as dark or rich.)
½ teaspoon baking powder
½ cup mini chocolate chips (optional)

1 full bag caramels, unwrapped
⅓ cup (¾ stick or 6 tablespoons) butter
3½ tablespoons of milk
1 cup chopped pecans

1. Grease a 9x13-inch pan.

2. Cream together the 1 cup of butter, sugar, eggs and vanilla.

3. Add the cocoa to the butter mixture and mix thoroughly.

4. Add the flour, baking powder and chocolate chips to the chocolate mixture and thoroughly mix for
   2 minutes.

5. Pour the batter into the prepared pan.

*continued on next page*

6. Bake for 25-35 minutes or until an inserted knife or toothpick comes out clean.

7. While the brownies are baking, prepare the topping.

TOPPING:

1. In a microwave-safe bowl, place the unwrapped caramels, ⅓ cup butter and milk. Microwave the caramels, butter and milk about 60 seconds, stir and then continue cooking in the microwave for 30-second intervals until all is melted and mixed together.

2. Immediately after removing the pan from the oven, drizzle all the caramel topping onto the hot brownies.

3. Lightly sprinkle the pecans over the caramel topping and, if not too hot, lightly press the pecans into the caramel topping with the palm of your hand. Immediately cover with cellophane or a plastic lid. Allow to cool prior to cutting into 9, 12 or 16 bars. Always keep each bar or the pan tightly covered with cellophane.

# Aunt Essie's Hershey Syrup Brownies

---

*This is my Mother's Aunt's recipe. I am the fourth generation this recipe has been passed onto.
On the rare occasions when my Mother baked from scratch, these brownies were usually what she baked.
I remember that when my Mother baked this recipe, the brownies never lasted longer than one day.
The icing works well, but I prefer using Aunt Lil's Aunt's Chocolate Icing (page 97). The choice of
which icing to use is yours—try them both and then determine which one you prefer.*

Preheat oven to 350 degrees F.

½ cup (1 stick) butter
1 cup sugar
4 eggs
1 tablespoon vanilla
1, 16-ounce can Hershey syrup
1⅓ cups flour
¼ teaspoon baking powder
1 cup chopped walnuts and/or chocolate chips (optional)

1. Cream together the butter, sugar, eggs and vanilla.

2. Add the Hershey syrup to the butter mixture and mix together thoroughly.

3. Add the flour, baking powder and walnuts and/or chocolate chips to the chocolate mixture and mix for 2 minutes.

4. Grease a 9x13-inch pan.

5. Pour the batter into the prepared pan.

6. Bake 30-35 minutes or until an inserted knife or toothpick comes out clean.

7. While the brownies are in the oven, prepare the frosting.

*continued on next page*

AUNT ESSIE'S FROSTING:
2 tablespoons butter
3 tablespoons milk
¾ cup sugar
¼ cup chocolate chips

1. In a saucepan, boil the butter, milk and sugar for 30 seconds or so.

2. While the mixture is boiling, remove from heat and mix in the chocolate chips.

3. Pour the frosting onto the brownies.

Or, use Aunt Lil's Aunt's Chocolate Icing (see page 97)/

# Patt's Favorite White Chocolate Brownies

*If you were ever to meet my dear friend Patt and ask her what is the best treat I bake,
she will no doubt say the White Chocolate Brownies. She lives more than 1,500 miles away from Colorado,
and whenever I call to see what she wants for her birthday, Christmas, the kids' birthdays, etc.,
to the end of time I will get the same response: Patt wants "White Chocolate Brownies" and the boys
want "Snickerdoodles." For all who enjoy white chocolate, this recipe is absolutely awesome.*

Preheat oven to 350 degrees F.

1 cup (2 sticks) butter
14 ounces white chocolate chopped into ¼-inch pieces or 1¼ bags white chocolate chips
1 cup sugar
4 eggs
1½ tablespoons vanilla
2 cups plus 2 tablespoons flour
1½ cups mini chocolate chips

1. Place the butter in the microwave and cook until thoroughly melted.

2. Add the white chocolate to the melted butter and continue cooking in the microwave for 1-2 minutes until all the white chocolate is melted. (Do not burn any of the white chocolate; you just want it to melt it into the butter.)

3. In a separate bowl, cream together the sugar, eggs and vanilla for 3 minutes.

4. Add the white chocolate and butter to the egg mixture, and mix for 2 minutes.

5. Gradually add the flour in portions. Make sure each portion is thoroughly mixed in prior to adding another portion of flour.

6. Add ¾ cup of mini chips, and on slow speed mix the batter thoroughly.

7. Grease a 9x13-inch pan.

*continued on next page*

8. Pour the batter into the prepared pan.

9. Sprinkle the remaining chips all over the top of the batter.

10. Bake 25-30 minutes or until an inserted knife or toothpick comes out clean. The brownies will sink a little in the middle. Allow to cool at least 10 minutes prior to slicing.

# Grandmom's Peanut Butter Bars

---

*Occasionally, I received a care package from my Grandmom when I was little and spent the summer at overnight summer camp. That package always contained these treats along with a variety of cookies. To my knowledge, this was the only time she baked these scrumptious bars. I had not tasted them for a few decades until one day, while I was searching through the treasures in her Tin Box, I came upon this recipe and immediately baked some up. Oh boy, did the forgotten memories of those summer days come floating back into my mind as I ate two bars within 20 minutes after these bars came out of the oven.*

Preheat oven to 350 degrees F.

⅔ cup (1⅓ sticks) butter
1⅓ cups creamy or chunky peanut butter
4 eggs
2 cups sugar
1 tablespoon vanilla
2¼ cups flour
2 teaspoons baking powder
1 cup mini chocolate chips (optional)

1. Cream together the butter, eggs, peanut butter, sugar and vanilla.

2. Mix the butter mixture for 3 minutes.

3. Add the flour, baking powder and half the mini chips, if adding the chips.

4. Grease a 9x13-inch pan.

5. Pour the batter into the prepared pan.

6. Sprinkle the remaining mini chips all over the top of the batter.

7. Bake for 30-40 minutes or until an inserted knife or toothpick comes out clean. Cool for 10 minutes prior to slicing.

# Oreo Crumb Cheesecake Bars

*Growing up in Philadelphia, I ate at several diners that served cheesecake. Some cheesecakes were OK and some were fabulous. For my birthday one year, my Dad sent me an astounding, 12-inch Oreo Cheesecake as a surprise. As wonderful as it was, I prefer a smooth cheesecake, not one with chunks in. Of course, friends and I ate the cake anyway. Nonetheless, that unexpected surprise gave me the idea for the recipe below. Not too sweet, not too rich, just right.*

Preheat oven to 350 degrees F.

THE CRUST:
⅔ box Oreo crumbs
2½ tablespoons melted butter
Reserve ½ cup plus 1 tablespoon Oreo crumbs for the topping, in a small bowl.

1. Grease a 9x13-inch pan.

2. With a fork, mix the remaining crumbs with the melted butter until the crumbs are just slightly moist. With the back of a large spoon or rubber spatula, softly press the moistened crumbs into the prepared pan, covering the entire bottom of the pan with the crumbs.

3. Bake the crust for 5-7 minutes; remove from the oven and prepare the filling.

FILLING:
2½ 8-ounce packages cream cheese
1 cup sugar
2 eggs
¼ cup milk
2 teaspoons vanilla

1. Cream together the cream cheese, sugar, eggs, milk and vanilla.

2. Remove the crust from the oven and spread the cream cheese batter onto the hot crust.

3. Sprinkle remaining crumbs over cream cheese batter.

4. Bake for 30-40 minutes or until the filling barely jiggles when the pan is slightly shaken.

5. Allow to cool 20-30 minutes, cover with cellophane and refrigerate for at least 3 hours.

If you want, add an Oreo to the top of each piece prior to serving.

# Success

To laugh often and much

To win the respect of intelligent people

And the affection of children

To earn the appreciation of honest critics

And to endure the betrayal of false friends

To appreciate beauty

And find the best in others

To leave the world a bit better

Whether by a healthy child

A garden patch or a redeemed social condition

To know even one life has breathed easier

Because you have lived

This is to have succeeded.

*Ralph Waldo Emerson*

# Pies

*\* All recipes can be doubled or tripled.*
*\* I always place my pies on a cookie sheet lined with foil to catch*
*any juice that may overflow from the crust.*
*\* All pies will serve six to eight people.*

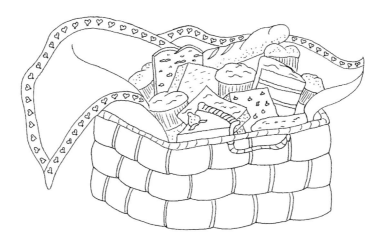

**Clockwise from top: Blueberry, Cherry, Apple Streusel**

# The Pie Crusts

*The most important aspect of making pie crust is to make sure the crust turns out flaky—not doughy and thick as a pizza crust tends to be. These recipes work anywhere, even in the Rocky Mountains. All the crusts taste marvelous and are wonderfully flaky.*

**For 9-inch round pans**

SINGLE CRUST PIE:
1½ cups flour
½ teaspoon salt
3 tablespoons water
½ cup plus 1 tablespoon shortening

1. Sift together the flour and salt.

2. Add the water to ¼ cup of the flour/salt combination and mix to make a paste.

3. With a pastry blender or two forks, cut the shortening into the remaining flour/salt combination until little beads begin to form.

4. Pour the paste into the flour/shortening mixture and, with a fork, work the paste into the mixture until manageable.

5. Form the dough into a flat ball and roll out onto a floured surface.

6. Turn the dough over carefully two or three times during the rolling process.

7. Gently lift and fit the dough into the pie pan.

8. Trim off any excess dough and either flute the edge or press the edge with the tines of a fork.

*continued on next page*

DOUBLE-CRUST PIE:
2 cups flour
1 teaspoon salt
¼ cup water
¾ plus 1 tablespoon shortening

1. Follow the same mixing and rolling procedure for the single pie crust, but divide the dough in half prior to rolling.

2. Have the top crust rolled out and ready to apply on top of the filling.

3. Tuck the edges of the top crust under the edge of the bottom crust, flute the edge and bake the chosen pie as directed.

LATTICE-TOPPED PIE:
A lattice-topped pie is a crust that is cut into strips and then placed in a woven or a crisscross pattern across the pie filling.

1. Follow the recipe for a double-crust pie.

2. After rolling out the circular top pie crust, cut 12 even width strips out of the dough.

3. Place the first 6 strips vertically across the pie filling and the second set of 6 strips horizontally across the pie filling and flute the edge. Then, bake the pie according to the given instructions.

# Low-Fat Pie Crust

♥

*Great for those on low-fat or low-cholesterol diets.*

This is a single pie crust recipe.
Double this recipe for a two-crust pie.

1 cup plus 1 tablespoon flour
2 tablespoons canola oil
1 tablespoon skim milk

1. Mix the 3 ingredients together thoroughly.

2. After mixing, place dough in a gathered clump on a lightly floured piece of waxed paper.

3. Then, place another piece of waxed paper on top of the clump of dough and proceed to roll out as with any other pie crust.

If these crust recipes seem too dry prior to rolling out, you can add an extra tablespoon of shortening.
I would not suggest adding more oil to the low-fat crust recipe; instead, add 1 extra teaspoon skim milk at a time to moisten the dough.

# Apple Pie

**SUGAR** (FREE)

*What would a baking recipe book be like without an All-American Apple Pie? There must be hundreds of recipes out there for this homegrown treat. According to legend, John Chapman, aka Johnny Appleseed, wandered throughout the United States, planting apple seeds. His journey produced apple trees in almost every state in our nation. For this reason, I dedicate this recipe to Johnny Appleseed. This recipe has yet to ever be turned down by anyone I served it to—even those who thought they did not like apple pie.*

**2-crust pie**

Preheat oven to 375 degrees F.

6½ cups apples (about 3¼ lbs.), peeled and thinly sliced
1 tablespoon lemon juice
¾ cup sugar or sugar substitute
2 tablespoons flour
2 teaspoons cinnamon
½ teaspoon nutmeg
2 tablespoons butter, sliced
⅓ cup of chopped walnuts and/or raisins (optional)

1. Prepare the crust. Gently place the bottom crust into a 9-inch pie pan and trim the edge. Roll out the remaining crust and have it ready to place on top of the apples.

2. Toss the apples with the lemon juice.

3. Stir together the dry ingredients.

4. Gently mix the dry ingredients with the apples to coat.

5. Spoon or pour the apples onto the bottom crust. Dot the apples with slices of butter.

6. Cover the apples with the remaining crust. Fold upper crust edge under the lower crust edge and flute the edge. Poke a few holes into the top crust with a fork. Sprinkle a teaspoon of cinnamon/sugar on the top.

7. Bake for 50-60 minutes. If the edges begin to brown too early, cover the edge of the pie with a piece of foil to prevent burning and continue baking.

# Streusel Apple Pie

*For those who enjoy streusel cakes, this recipe is the pie you're sure to enjoy. It has lots of the same ingredients as a traditional apple pie, but with a sweeter topping. This pie's enchanting appearance and aroma will make your guests' mouths water. This pie is sure to leave a lasting impression on all who experience its enticing sensation.*

Preheat oven to 350 degrees F.

**1-crust pie**

STREUSEL TOPPING:
½ cup brown sugar
¾ cup flour
1½ teaspoons cinnamon
⅓ cup cold butter, chopped into small pieces
¼ cup chopped walnuts or raisins (optional)
Mix all the streusel ingredients until crumbly and set aside.

FILLING:
4-5 cups Granny Smith apples, peeled and thinly sliced
⅓ cup sugar
1 tablespoon lemon juice
2 tablespoons cornstarch
1½ teaspoons cinnamon
¼ teaspoon nutmeg
¼ cup raisins or chopped walnuts (optional)

1. Prepare the bottom crust and gently place it into a 9-inch pie pan and flute the edge.

2. Toss the apples with the lemon juice.

*continued on next page*

3. Gently stir the remaining filling ingredients into the apples.

4. In portions, spoon the filling into the prepared pie shell.

5. Sprinkle streusel topping evenly over the apples.

6. Bake for about 40-45 minutes or until juices are bubbly. Allow to cool for about 15 minutes prior to serving.

# Cranberry Pie

---

*Cranberries are only fresh during the autumn months, hence a perfect time to bake this pie.
The ginger adds a bit of pizzazz to the berries and will fill your home with an irresistible scent that will send
your neighbors rushing over. This pie looks tremendously alluring on a Thanksgiving dessert table.*

**2-crust or lattice-topped pie**

Preheat oven to 350 degrees F.

1¼ bags fresh cranberries, cut into pieces (do not use a food processor)
2 tablespoons flour
⅔ cup sugar
½ teaspoon ground ginger
½ teaspoon cinnamon
1 tablespoon lemon juice
3 tablespoons butter, sliced

1. Prepare the bottom crust and gently place into a 9-inch pie pan. Roll out the remaining crust and have it ready to place on top of the berries. If using a lattice top, have the strips precut and ready to apply.

2. Toss the cranberries with the flour, sugar, ginger, cinnamon and lemon juice.

3. Carefully pour the berries into the prepared pie crust. Dot the cranberries with slices of butter.

4. Gently cover with the remaining crust or apply the lattice topping. Fold upper crust edge under the lower crust edge and flute the edge.

5. Bake the pie about 1 hour or until the crust is golden. If the edge begins to turn brown, wrap a piece of foil around the edge of the pie and continue baking. Allow to cool a bit before serving.

This pie goes great with vanilla ice cream.

# Grandmom's Blueberry Pie

*This pie has always been a great seller. I continue to get requests for it today and have been told by many that it is the best blueberry pie they have ever tasted. I wouldn't change this recipe for a stack of gold.*

**2-crust or lattice-topped pie**

Preheat oven to 375 degrees F.

5 cups fresh blueberries or two 12-ounce packages frozen blueberries
⅔ cup sugar or sugar substitute
2½ tablespoons tapioca
½ teaspoon cinnamon
1 tablespoon lemon juice
3 tablespoons butter, sliced
1 tablespoon milk

1. Prepare the bottom pie crust and gently place into a 9-inch pie pan. Prepare the top crust and have it ready to apply. If using a lattice-topped crust, precut the strips and have them ready to apply on top of the berries.

2. Toss together the blueberries, sugar, tapioca, cinnamon and lemon juice.

3. Pour the berries into the pie crust and dot with slices of the butter.

4. Gently place choice of top crust onto the berries. Fold upper crust edge under the lower crust edge and flute the edge. Brush the crust with a tablespoon of milk or water, using your fingers or a pastry brush.

5. Sprinkle a teaspoon of sugar on top of the crust and if using a whole pie crust, poke holes into the crust with a fork.

6. Bake for about 45-50 minutes or until the juices begin to bubble. If the pie edge begins to brown, cover the edge with a piece of foil and continue baking. Allow to cool for 30 plus minutes prior to serving.

# Cherry Pie

*I once had a customer who bought this pie from me and within 45 minutes bought a second cherry pie.*
*He said it was so wonderful that the first one disappeared before he could even taste it, so he needed another.*
*Full of zest from summer sunshine, this recipe can be made any time of year.*
*This is a pie that will light up any table that it is placed upon.*

**2-crust or lattice-topped pie**

Preheat oven to 350 degrees F.

6 cups dark, red cherries (fresh and pitted, canned, or frozen and thawed, drained)
½ cup sugar or sugar substitute
2 ½ tablespoons tapioca
1 teaspoon vanilla
½ teaspoon almond extract
3 tablespoons butter, sliced
1 tablespoon milk

1. Prepare bottom crust and gently place into a 9-inch pie pan. Prepare the top crust and have ready to apply. If using a lattice top, have the strips precut and ready to apply.

2. Toss the cherries with the sugar, tapioca, vanilla and almond extract.

3. Pour the cherries into the prepared pie crust and dot them with slices of butter.

4. Gently place the top crust or lattice top onto the cherries. Fold upper crust edge under the lower crust edge and flute the edge. Using your fingers or pastry brush, spread the milk over the crust. Sprinkle a teaspoon of sugar over the top and poke holes with a fork all over the crust, if not using a lattice topping.

5. Bake for about 45-50 minutes or until golden with the juices bubbling. If the crust begins to brown around the edge, cover the edge with a piece of foil and continue baking. Allow pie to cool for 30-45 minutes prior to serving, if you can.

# Grandmom's Strawberry-Rhubarb Pie

*I can't think of another way to bring in a summer of fresh fruit treats than with this delicious pie.
This pie has a burst of flavor that can light up your day, especially if it's a rainy day.
This pie is perfect to serve on the Fourth of July or to bring on a picnic.*

**2-crust pie or lattice-topped pie**

Preheat oven to 375 degrees F.

4 cups fresh rhubarb, cut into ¼-⅓ inch slices
1½ cups fresh strawberries, sliced
⅔ cup sugar
2½ tablespoons tapioca
1 tablespoon lemon juice
1 teaspoon cinnamon
2 tablespoons butter

1. Prepare the bottom crust and gently place into a 9-inch pie pan. Prepare the top crust and have the lattice strips precut and ready to apply.

2. Toss together the rhubarb and strawberries with the sugar, tapioca, juice and cinnamon.

3. Pour the fruit mixture into the prepared pie crust. Dot the fruit with butter slices.

4. Apply the lattice topping. Fold upper crust edge under the lower crust edge and flute the edge. Sprinkle a teaspoon of sugar over the crust.

5. Bake for 45-50 minutes or until juices are bubbly. Allow to cool for 30 minutes prior to serving. Best served cool.

# Peach Pie

---

*Many years ago, I discovered a wonderful place down the mountain to get fresh produce. I walked in one summer day and the scent of fresh peaches was so appealing that I had to buy a whole case. I had no idea what I was going to do with all those peaches until a day or two later. I decided to peel and freeze most of them and with the remainder I developed this recipe and made a few pies. Since that time, this recipe has been requested over and over again.*

**2-crust pie**

Preheat oven to 350 degrees F.

6 cups fresh, pitted, skinned and sliced peaches or 3 cans sliced light
  peaches, drained
½ cup sugar
2 tablespoons brown sugar
2½ tablespoons tapioca
1 tablespoon lemon juice
1½ teaspoons cinnamon
½ teaspoon nutmeg
3 tablespoons butter, sliced

1. Prepare and gently place the bottom crust into a 9-inch pie pan. Prepare the top crust and have it ready to apply to the top of the pie.

2. Toss together the peaches, sugars, tapioca, juice and spices.

3. Pour fruit into the prepared pie crust and dot the fruit with slices of butter.

4. Gently place the top crust on the fruit. Fold upper crust edge under the lower crust edge and flute the edge.

5. Bake for about 1 hour or until juices begin to bubble and crust is golden. Allow to cool for 20-30 minutes prior to serving.

# Grandmom's Fresh Peach Crumb Pie

*Once again, I bought too many peaches and had to use them all up before they went bad. As usual,
I did not know what to do with them all, so I dug into my Grandmom's Tin Box and pulled out this recipe.
Then, I remembered that, once in a blue moon, she would bake a Peach Crumb Pie—and I remembered how
good it was. So I made the recipe, reminisced about the glorious days I spent in her kitchen as a little girl, and
then my friend and I greedily consumed it by the next day. I found it amazing that we just couldn't control the
direction of our forks digging into this pie. Oh my, my, my, how sweet it is.*

**1-crust pie and a crumb topping**

Preheat oven to 400 degrees F.

CRUMB TOPPING:
½ cup flour
¼ cup sugar or sugar substitute
2 tablespoons butter
2 teaspoons cinnamon
1 egg yolk
Mix the ingredients with a fork until tiny pea-size balls and crumbs form. Set crumbs aside in a bowl.

FILLING:
5 fresh peaches, peeled and thinly sliced
¾ cup sugar or sugar substitute
2 tablespoons tapioca
1 tablespoon lemon juice

1. Mix filling ingredients together; cover and let the mixture rest for about 15 minutes to soak in
   the tapioca.

2. In the meantime, prepare the crust and gently place it into a 9-inch pie pan and flute the edge.

3. Pour the filling into the pie shell and bake for 30 minutes.

4. Remove the pie from the oven and evenly sprinkle the crumbs on top.

5. Place the pie back in the oven and continue baking for another 10-15 minutes or until golden or light brown. Allow to cool for 20 minutes prior to devouring.

# Special Peach Pie

---

*I found this recipe in my Grandmom's Tin Box, but I can't fathom where it came from. It was in handwriting I did not recognize and was on a very old, brown piece of notepaper. It may be my Aunt Gert's, for she and my Grandmom were the best of friends. All I know is that I added a little speck of spice and ooh, la, la, it turned out gloriously. This is an outstanding recipe to bake when showing off your baking skills to family and friends. Oh, will they be impressed as they savor every bite.*

**Lattice-topped crust**

Preheat oven to 400 degrees F.

¾ cup (1½ sticks) butter
1 cup sugar
3 tablespoons flour
1 extra large egg or 2 medium eggs
½ teaspoon cinnamon
2 teaspoons vanilla
1½ cans light sliced or halved peaches, drained of all juice or 2¼ cups fresh peeled and sliced or
  halved peaches
2 tablespoons sugar

1. Prepare the bottom crust and gently place it into a 9-inch pie pan. Prepare the topping and have the lattice strips precut and ready to apply.

2. Mix together butter, 1 cup of sugar, flour, egg, cinnamon and vanilla and set aside.

3. Place the sliced peaches into the prepared crust. Sprinkle the 2 tablespoons sugar on top of the peaches.

4. Lightly spread butter mixture over peaches.

5. Gently apply the lattice crust top. Fold upper crust edge under the lower crust edge and flute the edge.

6. Bake pie for about 15 minutes and then reduce the oven temperature to 325 degrees F and continue baking for another 45 minutes. Allow to cool completely prior to serving.

# Shoofly Pie

*While I was growing up, my father occasionally went to Lancaster County in Pennsylvania for business. One Saturday afternoon, he took me with him and we stopped at this little Amish restaurant for lunch and my first taste of Shoofly Pie. I never knew there was such a thing until that day—I thought it was just something served in cartoons. Well, years later, I still remember the look and taste of that scrumptious treat, but I couldn't find a recipe anywhere. So I began playing around with the required ingredients. It took me awhile to come up with my desired result. When this recipe looked and tasted as I remembered, I took slices of the pie on My Route. A customer said to me, "I didn't know that you made Shoofly Pie; I haven't tasted one in years. My Mom would put walnuts in it, but this is great!" I knew then that I had come up with a recipe for the real thing.*

**1-crust pie, recipe is for two pies**

Preheat oven to 350 degrees F.

1 ½ cups water
1 teaspoon baking soda
1 ¼ cups molasses
2 beaten eggs (do not use extra large eggs)
½ teaspoon cinnamon
½ cup chopped walnuts (optional)
½ cup butter
3 cups flour
2 cups brown sugar
1 teaspoon cinnamon
½ teaspoon nutmeg
½ teaspoon cloves
½ teaspoon ginger

*continued on next page*

1. Prepare the bottom crusts and gently place them into two 9-inch pie pans and flute the edges.

2. Boil 2 cups water, measure out 1½ cups, discard the rest and dissolve the baking soda in the 1½ cups water.

3. Add the molasses, eggs, cinnamon and chopped walnuts (if using) to the water and mix.

4. Pour the molasses mixture into the prepared pie pans.

5. Mix together the butter, flour, brown sugar, cinnamon, nutmeg, cloves and ginger until crumbly.

6. Sprinkle the crumb mixture all over the molasses, making sure the amount is equal between the 2 pies.

7. Bake pies for about 30 minutes or until filling is firm. Completely cool prior to slicing and serving.

# Grandmom's Raisin Pie

*Several years, ago my former accountant asked me to make him a Raisin Pie and I said "Sure,"
without having any idea what I was saying. I only remembered I had tasted one at my Grandmom's.
So I came home and searched her Tin Box. Gosh, did I ever think myself lucky when I found an old, browned
index card labeled Raisin Pie. My accountant loved this pie, as will any fan of lots of raisins.*

**2-crust pie**

Preheat oven to 400 degrees F.

2 cups raisins (1½ cups dark, ½ cup golden) soaked in hot water for 15 minutes
1 cup firmly packed brown sugar
3 tablespoons cornstarch
1½ cups water
½ cup orange juice
3 tablespoons lemon juice
1 teaspoon grated lemon peel or lemon zest
2 teaspoons orange peel or zest
1 teaspoon cinnamon
2 tablespoons butter, sliced

1. Prepare pie crust and gently place it into a 9-inch pie pan. Prepare the top crust and have it ready to apply on top of the filling.

2. Drain the water from the raisins and pat them dry with a paper towel.

3. In a large saucepan, combine the sugar and cornstarch. Add the water, orange juice, lemon juice, lemon peel, orange peel and cinnamon, and stir to mix. Add the raisins to the juice mixture.

4. Stirring frequently, heat the mixture over medium heat until it thickens and begins to boil. Continue stirring while boiling for one minute and remove from the heat. Stir for another minute and allow to cool to room temperature.

*continued on next page*

5. Pour the filling into the prepared pie crusts. Dot the top of the filling with butter slices.

6. Gently apply the top crust. Fold upper crust edge under the lower crust edge and flute the edge.

7. With a pastry brush or your fingers, spread about 1 tablespoon milk over the crust and, with a fork, poke holes into the top crust. Sprinkle a pinch of sugar or cinnamon sugar over the crust, if you like.

8. Bake for about 50-60 minutes or until the crust is golden. If the edge of the pie begins to brown, wrap a piece of foil around the edge and continue baking.

# Doc Tana's Favorite Pecan Pie

---

*For the life of me I cannot remember where I got this recipe. All I know is that it has been in my recipe notebook forever, and I have had this notebook for 18 to 20 years. It is a great pie. Not too sweet, not too tart, but just right. My vet, Doc Tana, loves this recipe and has yet to turn down a piece. It is also unbelievably easy to make.*

**1-crust pie**

Preheat oven to 350 degrees F.

2 ½ cups pecan halves
⅓ cup brown sugar
⅓ cup sugar
½ teaspoon cinnamon
3 eggs
1 cup light colored corn syrup
2 teaspoons vanilla
2 ½ tablespoons melted butter

1. Prepare crust and gently place it into a 9-inch pie pan and flute the edge.

2. Place all the pecans into the prepared pie crust and set aside.

3. Combine the brown sugar, sugar and cinnamon in a medium bowl until there are no lumps.

4. In a mixing bowl, beat the eggs for 30 seconds, add the corn syrup and vanilla.

5. Add the sugars and butter to the egg mixture and stir together until all the ingredients are fully incorporated.

6. Pour the mixture over the pecans.

7. Bake for 50-60 minutes until the filling is puffy or until an inserted knife comes out clean. Allow to cool completely prior to serving.

# Mom's Pumpkin Pie

*Everyone used to say my Mother made the best Pumpkin Pie. Growing up, when we had Thanksgiving at our house, and she had time, this is the pie she would make. My Aunt and Grandmom would make the other treats. This pie is one of the rare desserts she baked from scratch, and it was and still is worth every bite—even though I added nutmeg to her recipe. It is easy to make and is a marvelous pie for holiday entertaining or for an extra special treat anytime.*

**1-crust pie, recipe is for two pies**

Preheat oven to 350 degrees F.

6 eggs
2 cups brown sugar, firmly packed
4 teaspoons cinnamon
1½ teaspoons ginger
1 teaspoon cloves
1 teaspoon nutmeg
1 29-ounce can pumpkin
2 cups evaporated milk

1. Prepare pie crust and gently place them into two 9-inch pie pans and flute the edges.

2. Beat the eggs and then add the brown sugar, spices and pumpkin and mix. While mixing the ingredients, gradually stir the evaporated milk into the filling and mix completely.

3. Pour the filling evenly into the pie crusts.

4. Bake for about 50-55 minutes or until an inserted knife comes out clean. Allow the pie to cool completely prior to serving.

# Grandmom's Lemon Meringue Pie

*When I was a kid, my Grandmom would bring this to our house on holidays and sometimes just for a special treat. I thought it was majestic then, just as I do now. I was so thrilled when I found the recipe in her Tin Box. Even when she was in her early 80s, I can recall her specifically making this for me when she knew I was in town and would be coming over to spend time with her.*

**1-crust pie**

Preheat oven to 350 degrees F.

1 cup sugar
⅓ cup cornstarch
1¾ cups water
4 large separated eggs, yolks in a medium bowl and whites in a mixing bowl for the meringue
⅔ cup lemon juice
2 teaspoons lemon zest or peel
3 tablespoons butter (no substitutions)

1. Prepare the crust and gently place it into a 9-inch pie pan and flute the edge.

2. In a heavy saucepan, mix together the sugar, cornstarch and water. Over medium heat, stir the sugar mixture until it comes to a boil. Continue stirring at a boil for 1 minute.

3. Whisk half the sugar mixture in with the egg yolks and mix thoroughly.

4. Pour the egg/sugar mixture back into the saucepan with the remaining sugar, mix and bring to a boil. Boil the mixture for 2 minutes while constantly stirring.

5. Remove the pan from the heat and stir in the lemon juice, lemon peel and butter until the butter is fully melted and incorporated. Let the filling cool while making the meringue topping.

*continued on next page*

MERINGUE TOPPING:
4 egg whites, previously reserved
⅓ teaspoon cream of tartar
⅔ cup sugar, sifted 4 times and then measured
1½ teaspoons vanilla

1. Beat the egg whites with the cream of tartar until foamy.

2. Increase the speed on the mixer to medium-high, and add the sugar and vanilla. Continue beating the egg whites until stiff peaks form.

3. Fill the prepared pie crust with the lemon filling.

4. Spread the meringue onto the filling. Swirl the meringue with the back of a rubber spatula or spoon for a pretty effect.

5. Bake for 13-15 minutes or until meringue begins to turn a light golden color. Allow to cool completely prior to serving.

# Banana Crème Pie

*This is one of my favorite recipes in this book—a smooth, rich and creamy pie, just like it is supposed to be. One day a while back, while I was out, a customer picked up her pie without the whipped cream on top of the filling. I knew this customer, called her and asked her to bring the pie back so I could put on the whipped cream or give her another pie. She began to laugh and told me, "No need to worry," her husband, "already ate half of the pie without the whipped cream." Then she added, "this pie is sensational with or without the whipped cream". To me, it was one of the best compliments I ever received.*

**1-crust pie (prebaked crust)**

Preheat oven to 350 degrees F.

1. Prepare the pie crust and gently place it into a 9-inch pie pan and flute the edge.
2. Bake the pie crust 10-15 minutes or until golden. Remove the pan from the oven and set aside.

FILLING:
½ cup sugar
¼ cup cornstarch
2 ½ cups milk
1 ½ tablespoons vanilla
4 egg yolks, beat slightly beaten
2 ½ tablespoons butter
3 bananas

1. In a medium saucepan, thoroughly mix together the sugar and cornstarch.
2. Add the milk, vanilla and eggs to the sugar and mix with a rubber spatula, making sure all the sugar is incorporated and not lying on the bottom of the pan. Add the butter last, prior to cooking the filling.

*continued on next page*

3. Cook over medium-high heat, stirring constantly to prevent burning. After about 7-10 minutes, the mixture will begin to thicken. Just when it begins to boil, turn off the heat, remove the pan from the heat and continue stirring the filling for 1 minute.

4. Immediately cover the filling in the saucepan with a piece of cellophane to prevent a skin from forming. Allow to cool for 30 minutes.

5. Just before the 30 minutes are up, slice 3 bananas into ¼-⅓ inch slices and place them in the prepared crust.

6. Pour filling over the bananas and let cool for about 1 hour or until the filling reaches room temperature. Do not cover with cellophane.

7. Refrigerate at least 2½ hours prior to adding the whipped cream topping and serving.

WHIPPED CREAM TOPPING:
1 cup heavy whipping cream
1 teaspoon vanilla
2 tablespoons powdered sugar (optional)

1. In a mixing bowl, beat the cream, vanilla and sugar (if using) until stiff peaks form.

2. When ready to serve, spread the whipped cream topping over the filling. Swirl the cream around with a rubber spatula or the back of a spoon. Top with colored sprinkles, if you like.

Always put the whipped cream on the pie just before serving, otherwise it may begin to separate as if it is melting.

# Coconut Crème Pie

*This pie took a lot of work and experimentation. The first time I made it for a customer,
I put much too much coconut in the filling—and God bless the customer for telling me so.
So I began adding less and less coconut until I got what is said to be "a wonderful coconut crème pie".*

**1-crust pie (prebaked crust)**

Preheat oven to 350 degrees F.

1. Prepare the pie crust and gently place it into a 9-inch pie pan and flute the edge.

2. Bake the pie crust 10-15 minutes or until golden. Remove the pan from the oven and set aside.

FILLING:
¼ cup cornstarch
½ cup sugar
2½ cups milk
1 tablespoon vanilla
4 eggs yolks, beaten slightly
3 tablespoons butter
½ cup coconut

1. In a medium saucepan, completely mix together the sugar and cornstarch.

2. Add the milk, vanilla and eggs to the sugar and mix with a rubber spatula, making sure all the sugar is incorporated and not lying on bottom of the pan. Add the butter and 2 tablespoons of coconut to the filling last.

3. Cook over medium-high heat, stirring constantly to prevent burning. After about 7-10 minutes, the mixture will begin to thicken. Just when it begins to boil, turn off the heat, remove the pan from the heat and continue stirring for 1 minute.

*continued on next page*

4. Immediately cover the filling in the saucepan with a piece of cellophane to prevent a skin from forming. Allow to cool for 30 minutes.

5. While cooling, put the remaining coconut on a cookie sheet and bake in a 350 degrees F heated oven for a couple minutes until the coconut begins to brown. Immediately remove the pan from the oven and let it cool completely until ready to serve.

6. Pour the filling into the prepared pie crust and let cool for about 1 hour prior to refrigerating.

7. Refrigerate at least 2½ hours prior to adding the whipped cream and baked coconut.

WHIPPED CREAM TOPPING:
1 cup heavy whipping cream
1 teaspoon vanilla
2 tablespoons powdered sugar (optional)

1. In a mixing bowl, beat the topping ingredients until stiff peaks form.

2. When ready to serve, spread the whipped cream topping over the filling. Swirl the cream around with a rubber spatula or the back of a spoon. Sprinkle the baked coconut all over the whipped cream topping and serve.

Always put the whipped cream onto pie just before serving, otherwise it may begin to separate as if it is melting.

# Chocolate Crème Pie

---

*Yes, in case you are wondering, I did save the best pie for last. This recipe makes the most incredible*
***hot*** *chocolate pudding I have ever tasted. On more than one occasion I have made a batch and a half, simply*
*for the purpose of taking out about a cup of the filling and devouring it while it is hot. If you're a chocoholic,*
*such as myself, you will absolutely love this recipe. Furthermore, it is sure to make*
*quite an impression for all to whom you serve it—even yourself.*

**1-crust pie (prebaked crust)**

Preheat oven to 350 degrees F.

1. Prepare the pie crust and gently place it into a 9-inch pie pan and flute the edge.

2. Bake the pie crust 10-15 minutes or until golden. Remove the pan from the oven and set aside.

FILLING:
3 ¼ squares unsweetened chocolate
¾ cup plus 2 tablespoons sugar
¼ cup plus 1 tablespoon cornstarch
2 ¾ cups of milk
¼ cup heavy cream
1 tablespoon vanilla
3 egg yolks
2 ½ tablespoons butter

1. Melt the chocolate in a small microwave-safe bowl and set aside.

2. In a medium saucepan completely mix together the sugar and cornstarch.

3. Add the milk, heavy cream, vanilla and eggs to the sugar and mix with a rubber spatula making sure all the sugar is incorporated and not lying on bottom of the pan. Add the butter to the filling last.

4. Cook over medium-high heat, stirring consistently to prevent burning.

*continued on next page*

5. After about 7-10 minutes, the mixture will begin to thicken. Just when it begins to boil, turn off the heat, remove the pan from the heat and continue stirring for 1 minute. With a rubber spatula, add the melted chocolate to the filling and thoroughly mix the chocolate in until fully incorporated. (Now, put a big spoon in and taste it—only kidding.)

6. Immediately cover the filling with a piece of cellophane to prevent a skin from forming. Allow to cool for 30 minutes.

7. After 30 minutes, remove the cellophane, stir the filling and pour it into the prepared pie crust.

8. Cover again with cellophane and refrigerate for at least 2½ hours prior to serving with the whipped cream topping.

WHIPPED CREAM TOPPING:
1 cup heavy whipping cream
1 teaspoon vanilla
2 tablespoon powdered sugar (optional)

1. In a mixing bowl, beat all ingredients until stiff peaks form.

2. When ready to serve, spread the whipped cream topping over the filling. Swirl the cream around with a rubber spatula or the back of a spoon.

3. After spreading the whipped cream onto the filling, sprinkle the whipped cream with grated unsweetened chocolate or chocolate sprinkles.

Always put the whipped cream onto the pie just before serving, otherwise it may begin to separate as if it is melting.

# Banana Chocolate Crème Pie

*This variation of the Chocolate Crème Pie will forever remind me of eating frozen, chocolate-covered bananas at the beach when I was little. The rich and creamy chocolate filling tastes magnificent on top of the fresh bananas. Try it—you may like it!*

**1-crust pie (prebaked)**

1. Follow the recipe for the Chocolate Crème Pie on page 241.
2. Prior to pouring the filling into the prepared pie crust, slice 3 bananas into ¼-⅓ inch pieces onto the bottom of a prepared crust.
3. Pour the chocolate filling over the bananas.
4. Continue following the Chocolate Crème Pie instructions.

This pie is best served the same day it is made.

# Recipe for a Home

Half a cup friendship

Add a cup of thoughtfulness

Cream together with a

Pinch of powdered tenderness

Very lightly beaten

In a bowl of loyalty

With a cup of faith, one of hope,

And one of charity

Be sure to add a spoonful each

Of gaiety that sings

And also the ability to laugh

At little things

Moisten with sudden tears

Of heartfelt sympathy;

Bake in good-natured pan

And serve repeatedly

# Strudels

---

*Strudel is an elegant and delicious Austrian confection of thin dough wrapped around a filling and baked. The old way is to use sheets of phyllo dough, spread melted butter between each layer of dough, add the filling and then roll it up. Although phyllo dough sheets work and taste fabulous, I prefer to use a sheet of packaged puff pastry. I have found that puff pastry sheets work just as well and taste just as good, but are much easier to handle and much less time consuming. When making the following strudels, the choice of which thin dough to use is yours, unless specified otherwise. Either dough you choose will taste spectacular with any of the following fillings.*

*\* All recipes freeze well for up to eight days.*
*\* Most of the following recipes make two strudels.*

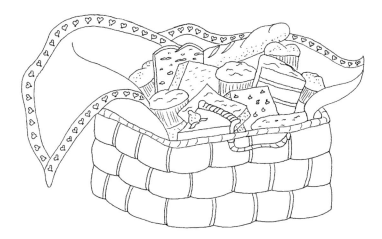

**Left to right:** Blueberry Cream Cheese Strudel, Apple Strudel

# Preparing Strudel Dough

For strudel, always use packaged puff pastry sheets (2 sheets) thawed, or use phyllo sheets thawed in the box.

If using puff pastry, remove 1 sheet at a time from the package, thaw and roll with a rolling pin to make it a bit bigger. Keep the second sheet in the refrigerator until ready to fill. Handle puff pastry as little as possible with your hands.

If using phyllo sheets, the sheets must be layered on top of each other with melted butter spread on top of each layer. Do not use more than 6 sheets per strudel, and cover the other 6 sheets until ready to use. Use no more than a ⅓ cup melted butter for each set of 6 sheets used in the layering process. Handle as gently as possible.

# Apple Strudel

*A friend's mother described this recipe as "absolutely delicious"!*

**Recipe for 2 strudels**

Preheat oven to 375 degrees F.

6-7 peeled and thinly sliced Granny Smith or Jonathon apples
⅓ cup bread crumbs
⅔ cup brown sugar
1 tablespoon cinnamon
1 teaspoon nutmeg (optional)
½ cup finely chopped walnuts or pecans (optional)
⅓ cup raisins (optional), soaked in water or brandy for about 15-20 minutes (Drain the liquid from the raisins prior to adding them to apples.)
1 tablespoon lemon juice

1. Greased 2 cookie sheets.

2. Mix all the ingredients together in a large bowl.

3. Prepare your choice of dough on a piece of waxed paper. I use puff pastry, but the choice is personal.

4. Add half the filling onto the lower long side of the dough, about 1 inch from the edge.

5. Using the waxed paper to help lift and roll the dough, tightly roll the dough and filling up like a jellyroll. Pinch the edge to seal.

6. Gently lift and place, sealed-side down, onto a greased cookie sheet.

7. Repeat with the remaining filling and dough.

8. Brush the top of each strudel with melted butter or brush the tops with an egg wash made from mixing together:

1 egg

¼ cup water

9. Cut 3 slits in the top of both strudels. Sprinkle a pinch of sugar or cinnamon/sugar onto the tops (optional).

10. Bake for about 45 minutes or until golden brown.

**Variation:**

APPLE CHEDDAR STRUDEL:

Omit half of the sugar (⅓ cup).

Add 1¾ cups grated cheddar cheese to the apples.

Follow the standard instructions.

# Kathleen's Mother's Austrian Strudel

---

*Kathleen was a friend's Mother and a great cook. From what she told me, she grew up in Germany, and her Mother grew up in Austria. When I went to visit her several years ago, she made the following recipe for me, knowing I appreciate a really good baked treat. I loved it immediately and requested the recipe before I even finished my piece. This recipe has been shared and enjoyed for more than a century, and I hope you find it as luscious as I did.*

**Recipe for 2 strudels**

For this recipe, use only phyllo dough.

1. Before you do anything else soak ⅓ cup raisins in 2 tablespoons rum for at least of 2 hours.

Preheat oven to 375 degrees F.

1. Thaw a 1 pound package of phyllo dough sheets in the box. Divide the sheets into 2 equal sets, keeping the extra set covered until ready to use. Melt ⅓ cup butter. On a large piece of waxed paper, using 1 sheet at a time, brush each sheet with a little melted butter. Use 6 sheets per strudel.

FILLING:
5 large cooking apples, such as Granny Smith or Jonathon, peeled and thinly sliced
Juice of 1 lemon
⅔ cup sugar
½ cup grated pecans or hazelnuts (filberts)
2 teaspoons cinnamon
⅓ cup sour cream

1. With your hands or a large spoon, mix the apples, juice, sugar, nuts, cinnamon and sour cream thoroughly. Add the raisins and rum and mix.

2. Place half the filling onto the lower long side of the dough, about 1 inch from the edge.

3. Tightly roll the dough and filling up like a jellyroll. Pinch the edge to seal.

4. Gently lift and place, sealed-side down, onto a greased cookie sheet.

5. Repeat with the remaining filling.

6. Brush the top of each roll with melted butter and cut 3 slits on the top of each roll.

7. Bake 40-45 minutes or until golden. Allow to cool for 20 minutes prior to serving.

# Cherry Strudel

*This is a great treat to take to a potluck or barbecue picnic—or just for something extra special. Full of cherries with a flaky crunch of a crust, this a perfect dessert anytime. Your family and friends will think you spent hours in the kitchen instead of only about 30 minutes. Delicate but hearty, all wrapped up. To me, a piece of this recipe, served warm with ice cream, is a piece of the good life.*

**Recipe for 2 strudels**

Preheat oven to 375 degrees F.

1. Use a whole package of puff pastry thawed; it holds the juice better. (Always keep the second sheet packaged and stored in the refrigerator until ready to use.) While puff pastry is thawing, prepare the filling.

FILLING:
7 cups dark, red cherries (canned or frozen and thawed)
2½ tablespoons tapioca
¾ cup sugar
⅔ cup ground almonds
½ cup bread crumbs
1 teaspoon almond extract
1½ teaspoons vanilla
1 tablespoons cold butter

1. After thawing the dough, place a sheet of puff pastry onto a greased cookie sheet and roll it out to make it a tad wider (do not roll to paper-thin).

2. Drain a little more than 1 cup of juice from the cherries into a small bowl and mix the juice with the tapioca. Cover the juice/tapioca and let it sit for a minimum of 15 minutes.

3. Mix all the ingredients together with your hands or with a large sturdy spoon. Add the juice to the ingredients and gently mix.

4. Place half the filling onto the lower long side of the dough, about 1 inch from the edge. Dot the filling with chunks from the 1 tablespoon of cold butter.

5. Tightly roll the dough and filling up like a jellyroll. Pinch the edge to seal.

6. Gently lift and place, sealed-side down, onto a greased cookie sheet.

7. Repeat with the remaining dough and filling and place onto a separate greased cookie sheet. Throw out any extra juice in the bottom of the bowl.

8. Brush the strudel tops with an egg wash made from mixing together:

   1 egg

   ¼ cup water

9. Cut 3 slits on top of each strudel.

10. Bake for 45-55 minutes or until golden. Allow to cool 20 minutes prior to serving.

This recipe goes splendidly with ice cream.

# Cream Cheese Strudel

*This recipe is so versatile that you could add almost anything to the cream cheese filling, and it will still taste fabulous. This variety of strudel has always been a favorite among my customers. Over the years, I have found that many customers enjoy this strudel made with fresh raspberries or blueberries, although I have been informed that the almond chocolate chip is exceptionally amazing. The choice of what to add to the cream cheese filling is yours. Try them all and then decide.*

**Recipe for 1 strudel**

Preheat oven to 375 degrees F.

Puff pastry dough sheets work best.

1½, 8-ounce packages cream cheese
¼ cup sugar
1 egg
2 teaspoons vanilla

1. Grease 1 cookie sheet.
2. Thaw 1 puff pastry sheet from the package and keep the remaining sheet in the freezer.
3. Place the pastry sheet onto a greased cookie sheet and roll a tad wider with a rolling pin. (Do not roll to paper-thin.)
4. Mix all the filling ingredients together thoroughly.
5. Spread the filling over the pastry sheet, leaving 1 inch from the top and bottom edges clean.

6. On top of the cream cheese filling, on the bottom third of the dough, add 1¼ cups of one of the following fruits or a mixture of any of the following fruits:

  **a.** fresh raspberries

  **b.** fresh strawberries

  **c.** fresh blackberries

  **d.** fresh blueberries

  **e.** fresh huckleberries

  **f.** fresh dark, red cherries
    fresh peeled and thinly sliced peaches,
    or sliced peaches canned in light syrup,
    drained and patted dry with a paper towel.

  **g.** For an almond or almond chocolate-chip strudel:
    mix 1 teaspoon almond extract, ½ cup chopped sliced almonds
    and/or ⅔ cup mini chocolate chips into the cream cheese filling
    and then spread over the pastry sheet. Sprinkle some chopped
    almonds on the top of the rolled up strudel.

7. Tightly roll dough and filling up like a jellyroll. Pinch the edge to seal. Roll it over to place, sealed-side down, on the prepared cookie sheet.

8. Brush the top of the strudel with melted butter or brush tops with an egg wash made from mixing together:
  1 egg
  ¼ cup water

9. Cut 3 slits onto the top of the strudel. Sprinkle a pinch of sugar on top of the strudel.

10. Bake for 45 minutes or until golden. Allow to cool completely prior to serving.

# Brie Bake

*Brie is a rich and creamy cheese. It has quite an elegant taste to it and is usually served with tiny pieces of bread, crackers, fruit or just as is. I happen to enjoy it much too much—so I often buy more than I need—and that's how I came up with the following recipe. I have made this recipe for company, friends, my ex and myself. This is a foolproof recipe. Anyone can make this recipe as long as they know how to turn on an oven and enjoy a little taste of what it feels like to be a king or queen.*

Preheat oven to 375 degrees F.

1 puff pastry sheet
1 chunk of Brie, at least 14-16 ounces (The Brie works better if the coating is
   removed and the cheese is frozen for 1-2 hours.)
2 tablespoons brown sugar or
   3 tablespoons huckleberry syrup or a few dabs of your favorite jam
¼ cup chopped pecans, hazelnuts or almonds (optional)

1. Place cold, almost thoroughly thawed, sheet puff pastry into a 9-inch pie pan. The sides of the pastry will overlap the pan.

2. Place the cheese in the middle of the puff pastry.

3. Sprinkle brown sugar, jam or huckleberry syrup and half the chopped nuts, if adding, on top of the cheese.

4. Fold the puff pastry to completely cover the cheese, pinching the edges together to seal as you go.

5. Brush the tops with an egg wash made from mixing together:
   1 egg
   ¼ cup water

6. If using nuts, sprinkle the remaining nuts on top of the pastry.

7. Bake for 20-30 minutes or until golden. The Brie will ooze its way out of the pastry shell a little bit, which is OK. Sometimes the Brie oozes out a lot—no matter, it tastes great anyway.

8. Serve immediately with a fork, crackers, French bread or fresh fruit.

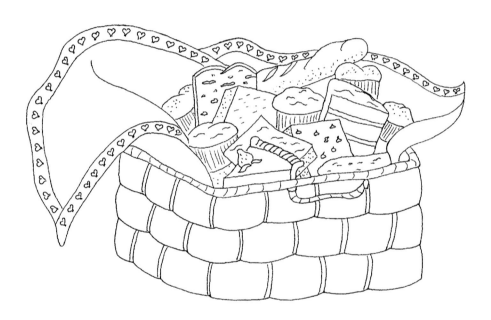

# Substitutions and Equivalents

One of the most important sections of a recipe book is the substitutions section. How many times have you grabbed for an ingredient halfway through mixing a recipe to discover you are out of it or never had it? This has happened to me more times than I can count. The following is a list of substitutions and measuring equivalents that can be used in the recipes found in this book, unless specified otherwise.

| WHEN RECIPE CALLS FOR: | YOU CAN USE: |
| --- | --- |
| **1 cup flour:** | ¾ cup + 2 tablespoons whole wheat flour, or for wheatless product, use ¾ cup + 2 tablespoons buckwheat flour mixed with 2 tablespoons quinoa flour. |
| **1 cup sugar:** | 1 cup minus 1 tablespoon sugar substitute such as Twin or Splenda. When measuring, measure the substitute just below the cup line, unless specified otherwise. |
| **1-lb. box powdered sugar:** | Equivalent to 3 ½ to 3 ¾ cups powdered sugar. |
| **1 tablespoon cornstarch:** | 2 tablespoons flour for thickening purposes. |
| **1 teaspoon baking powder:** | ½ teaspoon cream of tarter and ¼ teaspoon baking soda, for leavening purposes. |
| **2 ½ tablespoons tapioca:** | Only use minute tapioca in these recipes. This is equivalent to 5 tablespoons pearl tapioca soaked in water or mixed with 2 ½ tablespoons flour. |

*continued on next page*

**½ cup margarine or butter:**

½ cup is equivalent to 1 stick or a ¼ pound of butter or margarine. Unless otherwise specified they can be used in place of each other.

**½ cup melted margarine:**

Unless specified to use margarine only, ¼ cup of canola oil and ¼ cup melted margarine can be used instead of ½ cup melted margarine. For reducing fat and cholesterol: This does not apply to butter.

**1 cup canola oil:**

1 cup sunflower or safflower oil. Do not use corn oil, any other kind of vegetable oil, olive oil or peanut oil.

**1 cup milk:**

½ cup evaporated milk mixed with ½ cup water, soy milk, low fat milk or skim milk.

**1 cup buttermilk:**

Place 2 tablespoons lemon juice or white vinegar in a cup. Add enough milk to fill the cup **or** use 1 cup plain yogurt.

**1 cup sour cream:**

1 cup plain yogurt or 1 tablespoon lemon juice and enough evaporated milk to fill 1 cup.

**eggs:**

Equivalent amount of liquid egg substitute; check the container for equal amount. 1 extra-large egg is equivalent to 2 small eggs.

**1 teaspoon lemon zest:**

Zest is the grated rind of the lemon. One lemon rind grated will yield 1 teaspoon. One lemon, when fully squeezed, will yield just shy of 2 tablespoons juice; ½ teaspoon lemon extract is also equivalent to 1 teaspoon lemon zest.

**1 teaspoon or more of vanilla:**

Only use pure vanilla extract.

**1 cup soft bread crumbs:**

2 slices fresh bread.

**1 square unsweetened chocolate:** 3 tablespoons cocoa mixed with 1 tablespoon butter.

**6 cups peeled and sliced apples:** 6-7 large apples.

**6 cups peeled and sliced peaches:** 10-12 large peaches or 4, 15-ounce cans sliced peaches, drained of juice.

**3 cups sliced fresh rhubarb:** 1 pound fresh rhubarb.

**1 cup shredded cheese:** 4-5 ounces grated cheese.

**1 cup chopped walnuts and pecans:** Walnuts and pecans can be used interchangeably. 1 cup chopped equals 6 ounces.

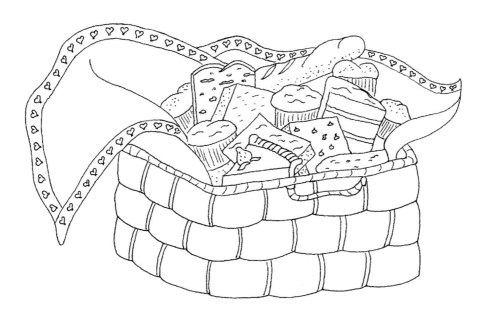

# *Index*

SUGAR *Sugar Free*
♥ *Low Fat and/or Low Cholesterol*

*continued on next page*

# Notes

# Notes

# Notes

# Notes

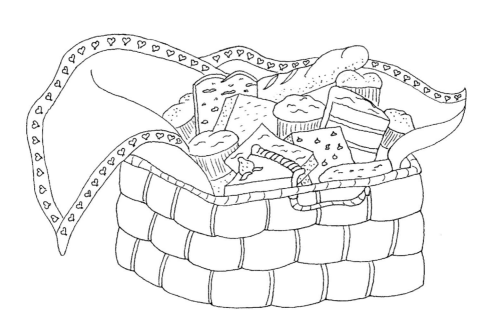